DYING FOR ATTENTION:
A GRAPHIC MEMOIR OF NURSING HOME CARE

© Susan MacLeod, 2021
First Edition
Printed by Gauvin in Gatineau, Quebec, Canada

Production and design by Colleen MacIsaac

Library and Archives Canada Cataloguing in Publication

Title: Dying for attention : a graphic memoir of nursing home care / by Susan MacLeod.
Names: MacLeod, Susan (Susan J.), author.
Identifiers: Canadiana 20210225114 | ISBN 9781772620610 (softcover)
Subjects: LCSH: MacLeod, Susan (Susan J.)—Comic books, strips, etc. | LCSH: MacLeod, Susan (Susan
    J.)—Family—Comic books, strips, etc. | LCSH: Nursing homes—Canada—Comic books, strips, etc. |
    LCSH: Nursing homes—Canada—Administration—Comic books, strips, etc. | LCSH: Nursing homes
    —Canada—Admission—Comic books, strips, etc. | LCGFT: Autobiographical comics. |
LCGFT: Medical comics.
Classification: LCC RA998.C2 M33 2021 | DDC 362.16092—dc23

Conundrum Press
Wolfville, NS, Canada
www.conundrumpress.com

Conundrum Press is located in Mi'kma'ki, the ancestral and unceded territory of the Mi'kmaq People

Conundrum Press gratefully acknowledges the financial support of the Canada Council for the Arts,
the Province of Nova Scotia, and the Government of Canada toward their publishing program.

 Canada Council   Conseil des Arts
for the Arts   du Canada
 NOVA SCOTIA
 Arts NOVA SCOTIA NOUVELLE-ÉCOSSE

This book is in part a work of remembering those long years with Mom.

It may not reflect the recollections of others.

" We have to decide
if seniors matter."

André Picard, Globe + Mail Health Columnist

FOREWORD

I see firsthand every day how much Dementia, Alzheimer's and the extremes of aging toward the end of life take so much from individuals and their families. The process of losing a parent starts long before death. Of the many challenges in navigating these diseases, the reversal of roles in the parent/child relationship and uneasy family dynamics contribute to an already challenging situation.

The very process of entering care is meant to alleviate some of the stress and workload but it is often fraught with guilt and fear as the adult child leads the process within an unknown and often confusing system. When a family acts together in a healthy partnership with the home, as well as sharing the burden between siblings, the transition can be smoother and more compassionate for everyone. Compassion is always key.

As a nursing home administrator, it was hard to read about the times when the system failed Susan and her mother. It is disheartening to see healthcare professionals demonstrate a lack of understanding on how to address death and dying. As the book shows, there is a larger system at play that can act in ways that discourages bedside compassion. At the same time, the excuses used by those on the front-line when the system fails people are demoralizing.

Please know we have wonderful, compassionate, and caring individuals who do their best every day despite the obstacles.

The message I took from Susan's reflections reminds me that doing our best is not the same as providing the best. It will take all of us: funders, government policy makers, non-profit advocates and associations, residents and family, developing the will and the means to work together to reform a system that, right now does not serve well, or all too often, even adequately.

I experienced Susan's passion to find answers and commitment to do better while working with her on the volunteer board of directors at Saint Vincent's Nursing Home. Those who know her would have no doubt she brought a creative lens to enhancing the lives of people living in long-term care. She pushed to think outside our comfort zone and to look to best practice examples from within our country and around the world.

Her approach to sourcing experts to guide her personal process was a call to action for me. It is her ability to reach out and access resources that is a reminder we should look for solutions and to not simply accept the status quo. If you see your own experience reflected in the pages, I hope you too will be invigorated to make change, no matter how small.

This population of elderly people deserves better because they themselves have served us much better when we were vulnerable. They are due more—much more.

— Angela Berrette
Executive Director, Saint Vincent's Nursing Home, Halifax, Nova Scotia

---

Editor's Note: Saint Vincent's is not the home where Susan's mother received her long term care. Saint Vincent's is a 150-bed non-profit home where Susan volunteered for six years and enjoys drawing Humans of Saint Vincent's on Instagram. www.svnh.ca

A NOTE ON GRAPHIC MEMOIR

Graphic memoir is a compelling medium combining pictures and words that together transcend what either format would be capable of on their own. Cartooning can allow for a perspective both nuanced and insightful and can bring levity to even the heaviest subject matter, using humour to open up difficult conversations in an accessible, honest way.

Susan MacLeod has done an amazing job of harnessing this medium in *Dying for Attention*, using her sharp insight based on a personal and multifaceted experience with nursing home care. Her expressive, playful drawings belie an incredibly nuanced storytelling style drawn from first-hand, visceral experience tempered with extensive research and self-awareness.

In 2007, comics artist and physician Dr. Ian Williams coined the term "Graphic Medicine". The term is now widely used to describe the highly effective role comics has in communicating a wide spectrum of healthcare experience (for more information on this term and work in this field, visit www.graphicmedicine.org).

This book is not only a stellar example of the ability of comics to speak to healthcare practices, but the ability of one individual's experience to act as a wayfinder for others navigating this complex — and often difficult — part of life. Susan has created a comic book that is an enjoyable, compelling read, a vulnerable and honest personal memoir, and a well-researched treatise on elder care in our society.

This story would not be the same in any other format and is a testament to the power of comics and graphic storytelling.

— Colleen MacIsaac
   Comic Artist
   littlefoible.net

CHAPTER ONE

I'VE ALWAYS DISLIKED OLD PEOPLE.

THERE WERE LOTS OF OLD PEOPLE AROUND ME.

YOU'RE LUCKY— YOUR KIDS HAVE ALL THEIR GRANDPARENTS IN TOWN.

RIGHT.

$1.29 2⁸⁹

WE WERE THE ONLY FAMILY ON THE BLOCK WITH BOTH SETS OF "OLDIES" IN TOWN.

WHAT TO SAY!

WHAT TO SAY?

PARDON, WHAT DID YOU SAY?

WHAT TO SAY?

A TYPICAL VISIT.

THAT HARPER! THE UTTER CONTEMPT OF THE MAN! OH!. HE DISGUSTS ME.

I'VE ALWAYS VOTED TORY!

OH, THE LUCKY PEOPLE WITHOUT GRANDPARENTS IN TOWN.

LATER.

WHAT ABOUT THAT SIDNEY CROSBY, BOB? HE'S GOING PLACES!

DON'T FOLLOW HOCKEY.

TIME TO GO!

HOP IN, DAD

DAD PREFERRED THE BACK SEAT.

YOU KNOW, I DON'T LIKE THE WAY THEY'RE TREATING THE OLDER PEOPLE AT CHURCH!

SLOW DOWN SUSAN!

THE MINISTER WROTE A LETTER SAYING WE NEEDED TO BE OPEN TO CHANGE —JUST TO US SENIORS!

YOU'RE TOO CLOSE TO THAT CAR!

JUST BECAUSE WE DON'T LIKE THE NEW MUSIC!

A YELLOW LIGHT AHEAD!

I CALL IT JIGGLY MUSIC. THAT LETTER WAS DISRESPECTFUL!

GO NORTH HERE!

TELL THE MINISTER WHAT YOU THINK, MOM. YOU'VE BEEN THERE A LONG TIME. YOU DESERVE RESPECT.

OH NO. HE WOULDN'T LISTEN.

SUSAN, YOU SHOULD ALWAYS TAKE A COMB WITH YOU. YOUR HAIR IS MESSY! I DON'T KNOW WHAT PEOPLE THINK!

YOU'RE TOO CLOSE TO THE CURB!

GRRRRR!

MOM STRUGGLES TO HOIST HERSELF OUT.

UGH! OOOH!

PHEW!

I WATCH THEM FUMBLE WITH THE LOCK . . .

. . . AND REALIZE MY PARENTS ARE **FRAIL!**

UNTIL THEN OLD PEOPLE WERE JUST ANNOYING TO ME.

I HAD IGNORED THE SIGNS OF DECLINE IN MY PARENTS.

I SHOULD HAVE REALIZED MOM WAS DEPRESSED.

LOOKING BACK NOW, I FEEL GUILTY I DIDN'T PAY MORE ATTENTION.

MOM NEVER DID LIKE TO COOK.

DAD VERY MUCH LIKED HAVING THINGS DONE FOR HIM.

I IMAGINE SHE WAS LONELY.

LET'S TALK ABOUT OUR MARRIAGE.

I TOOK AFTER DAD.

LET'S TALK ABOUT YOUR CHORES.

I DON'T DO CHORES.

CHURCH COMMITTEES WERE MOM'S ESCAPE.

I'VE CRUNCHED THE NUMBERS AND WE CAN AFFORD A DISHWASHER IN THE HALL.

Advent

BEFORE DAD, MOM WAS A HOSPITAL ADMINISTRATOR.

I'VE CRUNCHED THE NUMBERS AND WE CAN AFFORD A NEW OR.

EMERGENCY CODES

SHE ALWAYS WANTED ME TO BE INDEPENDENT.

NEVER DEPEND ON A MAN.

BE A SECRETARY.

DOES SHE KNOW THAT'S WAITING ON A MAN?

BUT NOT TOO INDEPENDENT.

I'M NEVER GETTING MARRIED!

YOU'LL BE LONELY.

I DID MARRY. AND REMAINED INDEPENDENT, IN FACT SUPPORTING THE FAMILY WHILE MY HUSBAND LAUNCHED A BUSINESS.

IT WAS BUSY.

I WORKED IN THE FRAUGHT FIELD OF GOVERNMENT HEALTH COMMUNICATIONS.

EVERYTHING'S FINE.

WE GAVE THE PUBLIC INFORMATION ABOUT HEALTH SERVICES . . .

. . . BUT ONLY INFORMATION THAT POLITICIANS WANTED HEARD.

LONG WAIT TIMES! WHY DID YOU WRITE THAT?

BECAUSE PEOPLE SHOULD KNOW?

ARE YOU MAD?

THIS GOVERNMENT ANNOUNCEMENT ABOUT JOB LOSSES WILL BE CONSIDERED SUCCESSFUL IF THE WORDS "JOB LOSSES" DO NOT APPEAR IN THE MEDIA.

WE GOT YELLED AT A LOT.

THE MINISTER OF HEALTH WANTS A SENIOR'S QUOTE IN THAT LONG-TERM CARE BROCHURE.

EEK! THE DEADLINE'S TOMORROW!

MY PARENTS LIVED IN THE LOWEST LEVEL OF CARE, THE LEAST NEED.

MOM, CAN I QUOTE YOU SAYING YOU'RE GETTING THE CARE AT THE RIGHT TIME?

SURE

WE BOTH KNEW IT WAS WRONG, BUT I WAS HER CHILD . . .

THANKS. SEE YOU LATER.

YOU'RE WELCOME.

. . . A FRANTIC WORKING MOTHER UNDER DEADLINE. MOM WANTED TO HELP ME OUT.

SEE ALL YOU WHINERS!

AND MY BOSSES ARE OFF MY BACK.

LONG TERM CARE IS GREAT

I HAD LITTLE OF HONEST COMMUNICATIONS TO DRAW UPON GROWING UP.

IN MY FAMILY, THE WORDS "GOOD QUESTION" OR "LET'S TALK ABOUT IT" WERE UNHEARD.

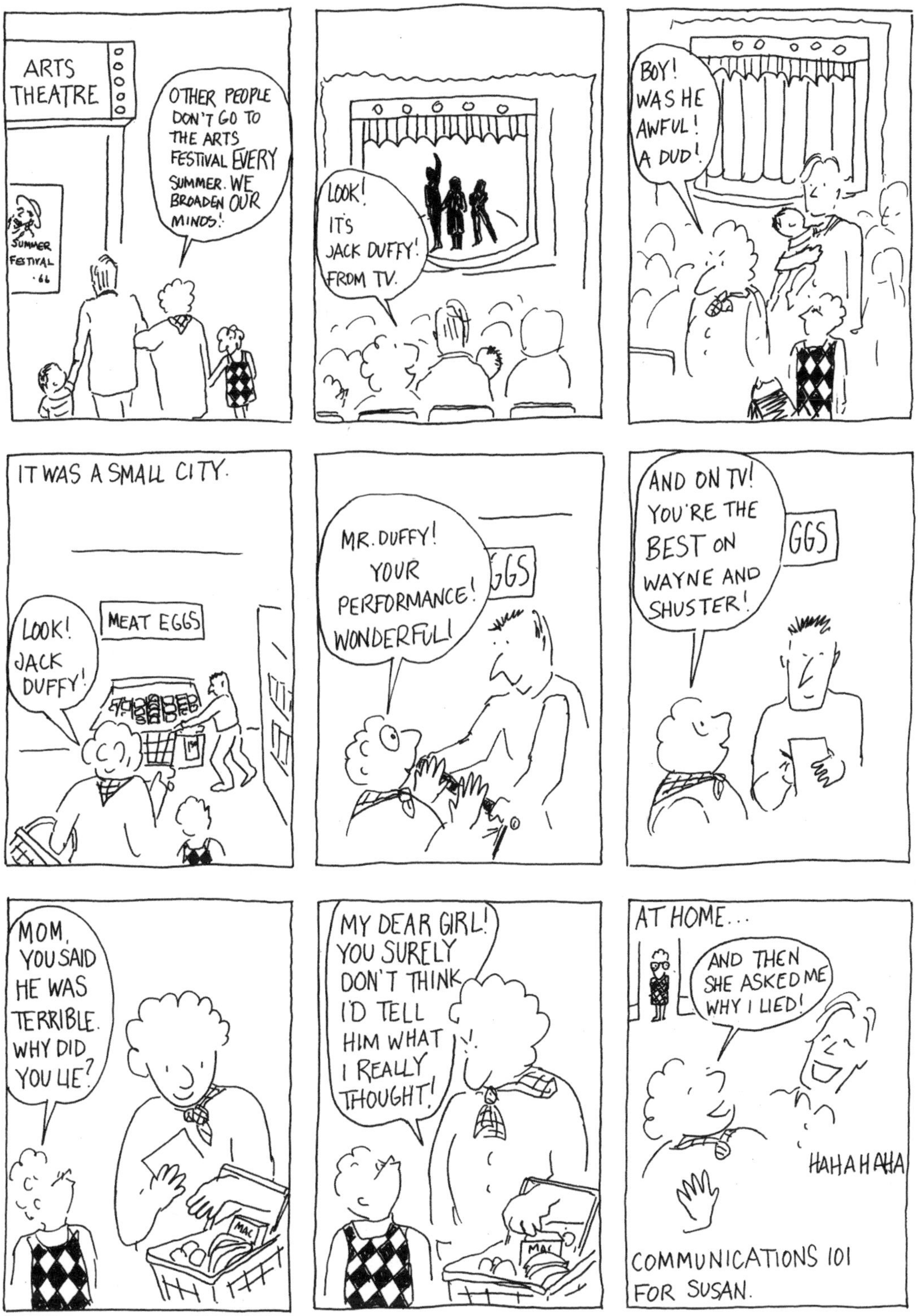
ARTS THEATRE
OTHER PEOPLE DON'T GO TO THE ARTS FESTIVAL EVERY SUMMER. WE BROADEN OUR MINDS!
SUMMER FESTIVAL '66
LOOK! IT'S JACK DUFFY! FROM TV.
BOY! WAS HE AWFUL! A DUD!
IT WAS A SMALL CITY.
MEAT EGGS
LOOK! JACK DUFFY!
MR. DUFFY! YOUR PERFORMANCE! WONDERFUL!
GGS
AND ON TV! YOU'RE THE BEST ON WAYNE AND SHUSTER!
GGS
MOM, YOU SAID HE WAS TERRIBLE. WHY DID YOU LIE?
MAC
MY DEAR GIRL! YOU SURELY DON'T THINK I'D TELL HIM WHAT I REALLY THOUGHT!
MAC
AT HOME...
AND THEN SHE ASKED ME WHY I LIED!
HAHAHAHA
COMMUNICATIONS 101 FOR SUSAN.

EVERY SUNDAY WE ALL MARCHED OFF TO CHURCH. WE ENTERED BY THE SIDE DOOR.

I HATE CHURCH!

WE ALWAYS SAT IN THE BALCONY, SAME PEW EVERY WEEK.

IT'S IMPORTANT TO KNOW WHERE YOU FIT. YOUR PLACE.

WE BELONG IN THE BALCONY.

ONLY THE MAYOR AND OTHER RICH PEOPLE SAT DOWNSTAIRS.

THIS PEW RESERVED FOR MUCKY-MUCKS.

MOM, BORN IN ENGLAND AND AN IMMIGRANT, KNEW ALL ABOUT STATUS.

WE'RE NOT UPPER CLASS, BUT WE'RE NOT LOWER CLASS. WE'RE LOWER-MIDDLE MIDDLE CLASS.

DAD AGREED.

DID YOU SEE? THE WIFE OF THE PRESIDENT OF SCOTT PAPER SPOKE TO ME!

WE LIVED AT THE LOWER END OF A LOWER-MIDDLE MIDDLE CLASS STREET.

MY PARENTS' PRIDE IN KNOWING OUR PLACE WAS STRONG.

BUT I KNEW WE WERE . . .

. . . WEIRD.

WHY ARE YOUR PARENTS SO DIFFERENT?

PTA

GOOD QUESTION. THEY DON'T DRESS OR EVEN LOOK LIKE OTHER PARENTS.

THEY WERE OLDER THAN OTHER PARENTS — AGE 39 WHEN I WAS BORN.

I THINK SHE HAS COLIC.

EITHER THAT OR SHE'S IN A LEG-HOLD TRAP.

I WAS THE BABY THEY THOUGHT THEY'D NEVER HAVE. SPECIAL!

ONE DAY I DISCOVERED I WAS TOO SPECIAL.

YOU'RE SPOILED ROTTEN.

WE'RE HAVING ANOTHER BABY TO FIX YOU.

THAT WAS A TYPICAL '60's PARENTING SOLUTION.

MOM! I HAD A NIGHTMARE! I'M SCARED!

OH GO BACK TO SLEEP! YOU HAVE NO IDEA WHAT FEAR IS!

UNDERSTANDING A CHILD'S PSYCHE WAS NOT A PARENT'S JOB.

I HATE PIANO LESSONS!

YOUR FATHER PLAYED PIANO! YOU WILL TOO!

MY BROTHER'S BIRTH ENDED THE "SPECIAL SUSAN" ERA. AND WE MOVED TO A NEW TOWN.

WEIRD.

DIFFERENT.

IT WAS PARTLY MY HAIR.

DO I LOOK LIKE HER?

GOD NO!

THE MOD SQUAD

IT BOTHERED MOM.

CONFORMING WAS IMPORTANT TO HER. PERHAPS BECAUSE SHE CAME FROM A WEIRD IMMIGRANT FAMILY.

AROUND THIS TIME, I STARTED BULLYING MY BROTHER. A BODYBUILDING MAGAZINE LEFT IN OUR APARTMENT WAS HIS FAVOURITE THING.

I HAD SKIPPED A GRADE AT MY LAST SCHOOL IN THE COUNTRY.

I WAS BEHIND IN SO MANY WAYS.

COMING FROM A ONE-ROOM SCHOOL HOUSE WITH 14 KIDS IN SEVEN GRADES...

YOU'RE SO CUTE!

... TO THE MEAN PLAYGROUNDS OF THE LARGE SCHOOL...

OUTTA THE WAY KID, OR I'LL KNOCK THE SHIT RIGHT OUTTA YA!

... WAS A SHOCK!

MY SHIT CAN BE KNOCKED OUT OF ME?!

NO ONE WAS ENCOURAGED TO PLAY NICE.

HERE SHE COMES! RUN!

AFTER SCHOOL ONE DAY, I CAME HOME AND SAW MY BROTHER'S MAGAZINE.

MUSCLE

WITHOUT EVEN KNOWING I WAS DOING IT...

MY DAD WAS HORRIFIED.

BUT SAID NOTHING TO ME— JUST GAVE ME A SAD DISAPPOINTED LOOK.

LATER

LOOK! A NEW TOY CAR...

...AND A NEW MAGAZINE!

I STOPPED PAYING ANY ATTENTION TO MY BROTHER.

AFTER ALL HE TAKES EVERYTHING

TAKE! TAKE! TAKE!

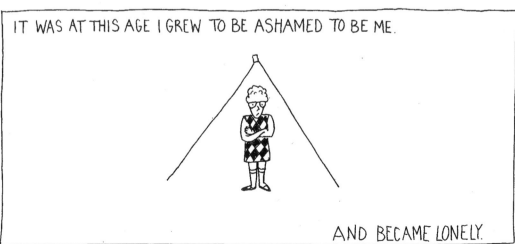

IT WAS AT THIS AGE I GREW TO BE ASHAMED TO BE ME.

AND BECAME LONELY.

I BECAME VERY SHY. THE ONE GOOD FRIEND I MADE TURNED OUT TO BE MEAN.

TELL ME WHAT YOU THINK OF KATHY.

KATHY'S NICE.

NO. WHAT DO REALLY THINK OF KATHY - LIKE HOW SHE LOOKS.

SHE LOOKS FINE.

COME ON! ONE THING YOU DON'T LIKE ABOUT HER!

WELL, HER EYES ARE FAR APART.

YEAH?! WELL YOUR HAIR'S FRIZZY!

KATHY WAS AT NANCY'S LISTENING IN. THEY NEVER SPOKE TO ME AGAIN.

I SPENT A LOT OF MY HIGH SCHOOL YEARS NOT RISKING REJECTION. I STAYED HOME ALONE READING MOM'S WOMEN'S MAGAZINES.

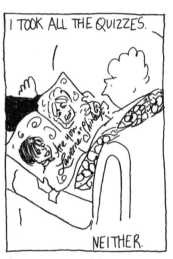

I TOOK ALL THE QUIZZES.

NEITHER.

DO YOU HAVE A MENTAL HEALTH PROBLEM?

I DID!

THE MAGAZINE SAYS I NEED TO GO TO A THERAPIST!

TAKE ME TO ONE!

MY MOTHER CANCELLED THE SUBSCRIPTION, AND WE DIDN'T SPEAK OF IT AGAIN.

COMMUNICATIONS 102 FOR SUSAN.

I NEVER SPOKE TO MY BROTHER EXCEPT TO BEAT HIM UP. IT FELT SO VISCERALLY SATISFYING TO SUBJUGATE HIM. HE JUST TOOK IT.

MY PARENTS DIDN'T SAY A WORD.

UNSPOKEN TENSION WAS A PRESENCE IN MY FAMILY.

I GUESS IT KEPT US SAFE UNTIL...

MR. MacLEOD. YOU HAVE PROSTATE CANCER AND YOUR HEART IS VERY COMPROMISED. YOU'RE TOO OLD TO TREAT.

I KNEW NOTHING OF THIS. BUT I SAW HIS HEALTH BEGIN TO FAIL.

EMERGENCY

FALSE ALARM.

THANK YOU FOR PICKING US UP.

EMERGENCY

FALSE ALARM.

THANK YOU FOR PICKING US UP.

EMERGEN

FALSE ALARM.

THANK YOU FOR PICKING US UP.

OK. MOM AND DAD. WHAT'S GOING ON!?

NOTHING!

SOMETHING'S GOING ON.

IT'S NO SURPRISE THAT EVEN IN CRISIS WE ALL PRETENDED THINGS WERE FINE.

SUSAN, YOUR DAD FELL IN THE NIGHT.

9:00AM

CAN YOU COME AND HELP ME GET HIM UP?

I'll BE RIGHT THERE! WHY DIDN'T YOU CALL ME SOONER?!

OH, I DIDN'T WANT TO BOTHER YOU.

ANOTHER DAY...

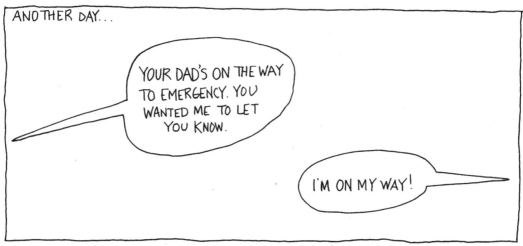

YOUR DAD'S ON THE WAY TO EMERGENCY. YOU WANTED ME TO LET YOU KNOW.

I'M ON MY WAY!

ONLY IF YOU'RE NOT TOO BUSY.

EMERGENC[Y]

AMBULANCE

BUT SHE HAD WAITED TOO LONG TO CALL EITHER ME OR THE AMBULANCE.

AMBULANCE BAY →

CHAPTER TWO

AND I'VE ALWAYS DISLIKED DEATH.

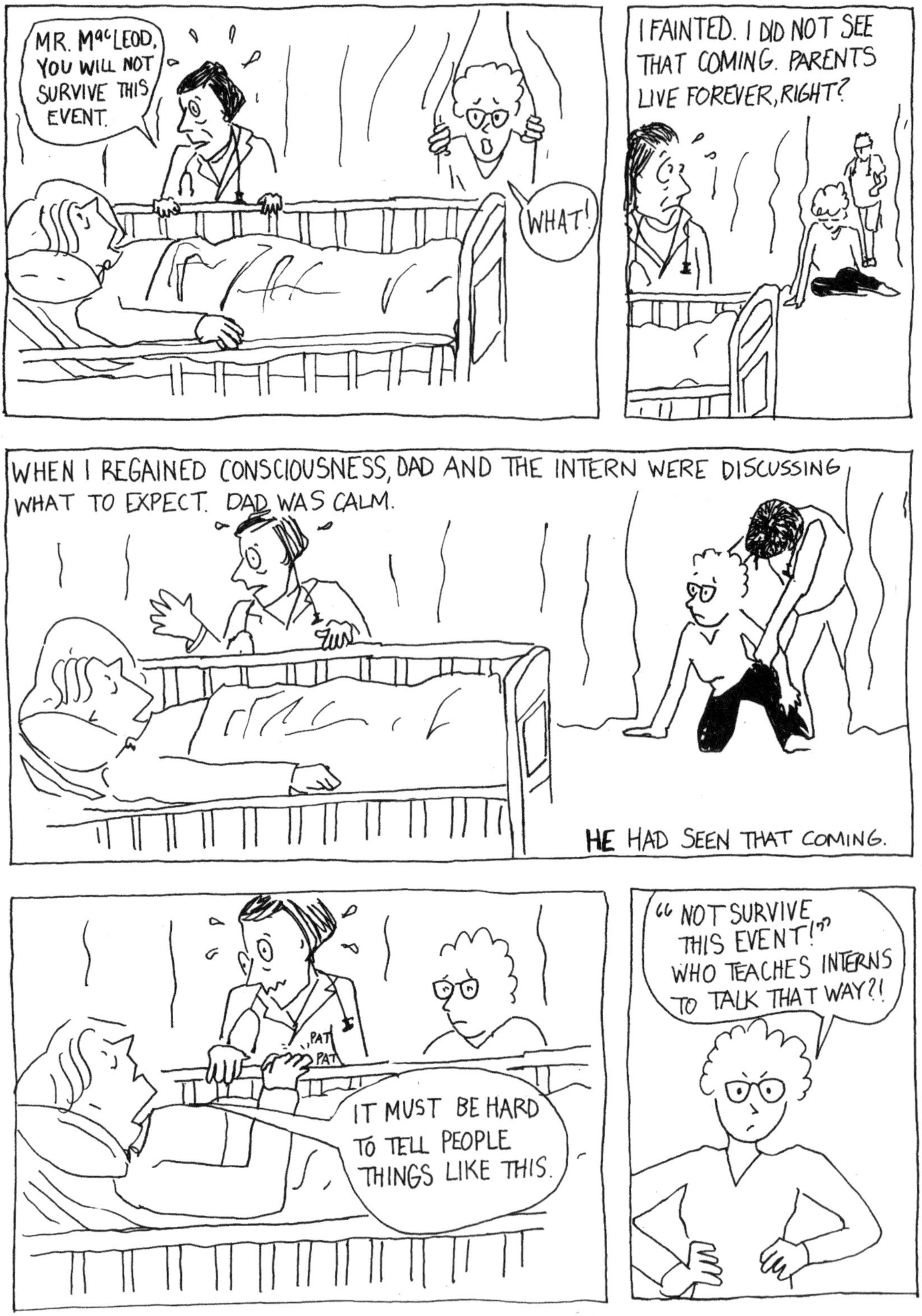
MR. MacLEOD, YOU WILL NOT SURVIVE THIS EVENT.
WHAT!
I FAINTED. I DID NOT SEE THAT COMING. PARENTS LIVE FOREVER, RIGHT?
WHEN I REGAINED CONSCIOUSNESS, DAD AND THE INTERN WERE DISCUSSING WHAT TO EXPECT. DAD WAS CALM.
HE HAD SEEN THAT COMING.
PAT PAT
IT MUST BE HARD TO TELL PEOPLE THINGS LIKE THIS.
"NOT SURVIVE THIS EVENT!" WHO TEACHES INTERNS TO TALK THAT WAY?!

DAD DIED THE WAY WE ALL HOPE TO BUT LIKELY WON'T.

SO. THIS IS THE END OF THE ROAD.

SHOULD I GET MOM?

NO. LET HER SLEEP. TELL HER IN THE MORNING.

I'VE THOUGHT ABOUT THIS, YOU KNOW. I'D LIKE DOUG TO SING THE SOLO — THE LAST CHORD.

AND NO PHOTO WITH THE OBIT!

WHY NOT?

I SAID NO!

FOR THE FUNERAL BULLETIN, I'D LIKE THE POEM THAT HAS THIS FIRST STANZA . . .

WHEN GROWN WEARY WITH CARE AND STRIFE
OUR LOVED ONES FIND IN SLEEP
THE PEACE THEY CRAVE.

WE SHOULD NOT WEEP
BUT LEARN TO COUNT
THIS LIFE
A PRELUDE TO THE ONE
THAT LIES BEYOND
THE GRAVE.

I'LL FIND THE REST OF THAT POEM, DAD.

I LOVE YOU.

I COULD NOT FIND THE REST OF THAT POEM.

THIS IS THE DRAWING I DID THEN BUT STOPPED BECAUSE IT FELT DISRESPECTFUL.

BUT HERE I AM PUBLISHING IT.

MY HUSBAND AND I SAT WITH DAD, UNCONSCIOUS, THROUGH THE NIGHT. AT 5:30 AM. WE WENT HOME TO REST — NO HOSPITAL COTS OR COMFORT.

I CALLED MY BROTHER MANY TIMES BUT HE DIDN'T PICK UP. HE'S HOURS BEHIND US, FAST ASLEEP.

WHY DOESN'T HE HAVE VOICEMAIL?

WE RETURN WITH MOM AT 9:00 AM.

NO CHANGE. BUT HE WOKE UP ONCE AND WAS FRIGHTENED TO FIND YOU GONE.

THAT MEMORY HAUNTS ME STILL.

AND WHO TEACHES THEM TO TALK TO FAMILIES THAT WAY?

MY BROTHER FINALLY PICKED UP THE PHONE AND ARRANGED THE LONG FLIGHT HOME. LATER...

MOM! HE'S COLD AND BLUE.

I KNOW! THEY KEEP IT TOO COLD IN HERE! THEY SHOULD BRING BLANKETS!

BLAME. DENIAL.

AT 7:00 PM DAD DIED. MY BROTHER'S FLIGHT TOUCHED DOWN.

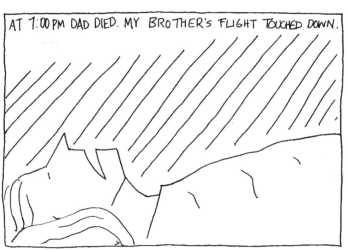

FORTY MINUTES LATER HE ARRIVED AT THE HOSPITAL.

WHO DOESN'T HAVE VOICEMAIL? FOR GAWD'S SAKE!

THEN A WEIRD CONVERSATION HAPPENED WITH THE DOCTOR.

I'M SORRY FOR YOUR LOSS MRS. MacLEOD.

THANK YOU.

DID HE GIVE HIS PERMISSION TO DONATE HIS ORGANS?

WELL YES! BUT HE'S 88! HIS ORGANS ARE TOO OLD!

I KNOW. I'M REQUIRED BY LAW TO ASK.

BUT IF YOU CAN USE THEM, DO!

IT'S FINE. I HAD TO ASK.

BUT HE'S TOO OLD!

I'M SORRY FOR YOUR LOSS.

THANK YOU.

FAMILY ROOM

AT THE BURIAL, AS THE ASHES WERE COMMITTED, I HEARD DAD.

I'M OK

THANKS DAD

I REALLY DID HEAR HIM.

I WORRIED ABOUT MOM AFTER EVERYONE HAD GONE HOME.

I NEEDN'T HAVE.

MOM SEEMED TO GAIN A NEW LEASE ON LIFE. SHE TOOK MY COUSIN, MY HUSBAND, MY DAUGHTER AND ME ON A GRAND VACATION WITH MY DAD'S WWII PENSION — TO BERMUDA!

DAD HAD BEEN A FEARFUL TRAVELLER.

WITH HELP, SHE DID EVERYTHING SHE WANTED TO THERE.

BUT EVERY MORNING...

DAD HELPED YOU OUT OF THE TUB FOR TWO YEARS?!

DAD HAD DONE A LOT.

I BECAME MUCH MORE KINDLY TO MOM.

TAKE IT EASY. ONE STEP AT A TIME.

I'M FINE!

IT WAS CLEAR SHE NEEDED MORE HELP.

DO YOU WANT ME TO GET YOU GROCERIES?

NO, I DON'T EAT.

SHE HAD TROUBLE WALKING BACK AND FORTH TO THE BUILDING'S COMMON ROOM, EVEN USING THE RAMP.

PANT PANT

AND HAD MORE PAIN. A LOT MORE.

MOM, THE DOCTOR SAID YOU COULD TAKE TYLENOL.

NO! I DON'T TAKE PILLS! I'M FINE!

IT WASN'T HARD TO CONVINCE MOM TO MOVE TO A HIGHER LEVEL OF CARE! SHE LOVED MOVING! ONCE, SHE AND DAD MOVED FOUR TIMES IN THREE YEARS. SHE COULD GET HER TEETH INTO A MOVING PROJECT.

OK!

MOM, I'M WONDERING ABOUT ASSISTED LIVING FOR YOU?

MOM LOVED A PROJECT. SHE WAS HIGHLY INTELLIGENT AND NEVER AFRAID TO STEP UP.

THERE WAS MORE TO HER THAN MET THE EYE.

CONGRATULATIONS, MISS JONES. YOU'RE GOING RIGHT INTO A SUPERVISORY ROLE.

RN GRADUATION DAY

MARJORIE, WE WANT YOU TO ATTEND THE NATIONAL CONFERENCE AS THIS REGION'S CHIEF DELEGATE.

SHE WAS AN AVID STUDENT OF HISTORY.

YOU'RE MISTAKEN. MARY STUART WAS JAILED AT LOCH LEVEN FIRST, NOT THE TOWER.

ONE TIME...

WHAT!! A GRAND PRIX RACE THROUGH OUR HISTORIC DOWNTOWN!

NEVER!

MARY! LET'S DO SOMETHING!

FRIEND MARY

PUBLIC CONSULATION

CONSIDER THE MOTHERS WITH STROLLERS TRYING TO CROSS THE STREETS!

YEAH!

(ME.)

THE RACE WENT AHEAD.

WE ALL KNOW YOU CAN'T BEAT CITY HALL.

BUT MOM AND I THOUGHT WE HAD A SHOT NAVIGATING...

... THE LONG-TERM CARE SYSTEM!

CAN'T SEE YOU.

GO HOME!

TAKE A NUMBER!

ENTHUSED TO HAVE A MOVING PROJECT, MOM SET ABOUT GETTING ASSESSED FOR ASSISTED LIVING.

YOU'VE REACHED THE OFFICES OF DOCTORS NORTH, MINOR, JONES, AUBREY, PATEL, WILSON, DODGE, AUCOIN, DODGE AND JUAN.

YOUR CALL IS IMPORTANT TO US. PLEASE LISTEN CAREFULLY AS OUR MENU HAS RECENTLY CHANGED.

FOR DOCTORS NORTH, MINOR, JONES, AUBREY AND PATEL, PLEASE PRESS ONE.

FOR DOCTORS WILSON, DODGE, AUCOIN, DODGE AND JUAN, PLEASE PRESS TWO.

FOR BLOOD TEST RESULTS, UPDATES ON WAIT TIMES, SPECIALIST REFERRALS, AND TO HOLD FOR THE RECEPTIONIST, PLEASE PRESS THREE.

FOR...

SLAMMMMM!

MY DOCTOR'S A QUACK! YOU KNOW, HE KILLED WYN WEST'S HUSBAND LAST YEAR!

SUSAN THE PROFESSIONAL TO THE RESUE!

I'll DO IT!

... THE OFFICES OF DOCTORS NORTH, MINOR, JONES, AUBREY, PATEL, WILSON, DODGE, AUCOIN, DODGE AND JUAN.

YOUR CALL IS IMPORTANT TO US. PLEASE LISTEN CAREFULLY AS OUR MENU HAS RECENTLY CHANGED.

KNOCK KNOCK

FOR DOCTORS NORTH, MINOR, JONES, AUBREY AND PATEL, PLEASE PRESS ONE...

THE MINISTER OF HEALTH WANTS A BRIEFING NOTE ON THIS...

TO HEAR THE MENU AGAIN...

...WITHIN THE HOUR.

THAT WAS JUST THE FIRST CALL. AFTER THAT CAME MOBILITY AIDS, FINANCIAL AID, POWER OF ATTORNEY, PACKING, MOVING, PAPERWORK FOR THE HOME ON TOP OF MY OWN DEADLINE-DRIVEN JOB, I ALSO HAD THE LION'S SHARE OF RESPONSIBILITY FOR OUR TEENAGERS, THE HOUSE-HOLD SHOPPING, SHOPPING FOR MOM. EATING. SLEEPING

YOU DON'T HAVE TO BE OVER 90 TO BE OVERWHELMED.

QUACKS!

SLAMMMMM!

SYSTEMS THAT MAKE HUMANS INHUMANE

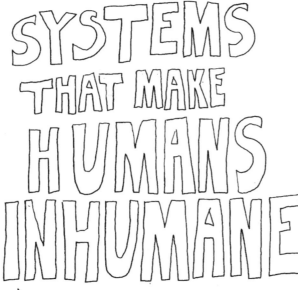

HOSPITAL WORKERS HAVE TO PROVIDE SPACE FOR THE FRAIL ELDERLY WHO NO LONGER NEED HOSPITAL CARE BUT ARE TOO FEEBLE TO GO BACK HOME, EVEN WITH A CAREGIVER.

NURSING HOME SPACE IS SCARCE. THE ELDERLY CAN WAIT IN HOSPITAL FOR SIX MONTHS OR MORE. THEY'RE CALLED

BED BLOCKERS!

RENLY.

ONCE YOU'RE IN THE SYSTEM, LITTLE IS HUMANIZED. I SAW THAT EVERY DAY WHEN I WORKED AT THE HOSPITAL IN MARKETING AND COMMUNICATIONS.

DETOUR   DETOUR

I JUST RAN INTO ANOTHER PERSON LOST IN THE BASEMENT.

OUR SLOGAN SHOULD BE "CONFUSE-A-PATIENT."

WE LIKED TO LOSE PEOPLE.

MY MOTHER IS IN ROOM 350 BUT THE NUMBERS GO FROM 200 TO 65.

WELL, YOU'VE ENTERED ANOTHER BUILDING. GO BACK DOWN THAT CORRIDOR.

I HAVE AN APPOINTMENT AT THE HEALTH SCIENCES CENTRE IN 15 MINUTES.

WHICH BUILDING?

HOSPITAL RECEPTION

THERE'S MORE THAN ONE!?

NINE. ALL OVER THE CITY.

HOSPITAL RECEPTION

MY CO-WORKER AND I TRIED TO MAKE CHANGES.

PETER, COULD YOU PLEASE MAKE A SIGN FOR THE ELEVATOR SAYING THE EXIT IS ON FLOOR 'ONE' AND 'MAIN' WILL TAKE YOU TO THE BASEMENT?

WE TRIED THAT ONCE BUT IT GOT SCRATCHED OFF. AND YOU'RE IN COMMUNICATIONS! NOT MY BOSS!!

MY COLLEAGUE AND I GAVE UP.

THEY PUT A MAN ON THE MOON.

AND THEN THERE WERE THE PHYSICAL SYSTEMS: OLD.

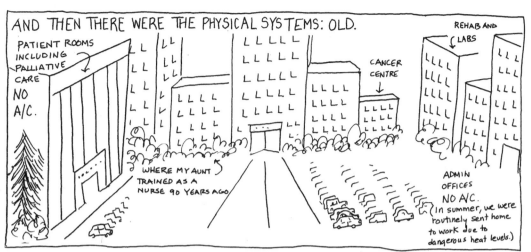

PATIENT ROOMS INCLUDING PALLIATIVE CARE

NO A/C.

WHERE MY AUNT TRAINED AS A NURSE 90 YEARS AGO

CANCER CENTRE

REHAB AND LABS

ADMIN OFFICES
NO A/C.
(In summer, we were routinely sent home to work due to dangerous heat levels.)

UNDERGROUND TUNNELS LINKED THE BUILDINGS.

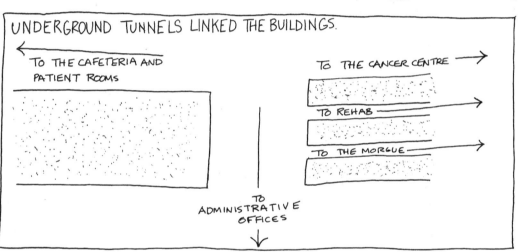

← TO THE CAFETERIA AND PATIENT ROOMS

TO THE CANCER CENTRE →

TO REHAB →

TO THE MORGUE →

TO ADMINISTRATIVE OFFICES ↓

ON THE WAY TO THE CAFETERIA, WE'D SEE DEAD BODIES BEING ROLLED TO THE MORGUE.

AHHHH!

MY FIRST TIME

I GOT USED TO IT LIKE EVERYONE ELSE.

← COFFEE

CANCER CENTRE →
MORGUE

IT WAS WORSE FOR THE LIVE CANCER PATIENTS.

← COFFEE

CANCER CENTRE →
MORGUE

AS FOR DEAD BODIES, I GOT ZEN.

IT'S GOOD TO WORK WHERE DEATH IS PRESENT.

WAKES US UP!

OM.

UNTIL ONE DAY...

MY MOTHER'S
GOING TO DIE.

CHAPTER THREE

MYSELF, I'VE ALWAYS FELT DISLIKED

I WAS SURPRISED TO FIND MYSELF UPSET BY THE THOUGHT OF MY MOTHER'S DEATH.

IT'S NOT AS IF WE LOVED EACH OTHER'S COMPANY.

MY TYPICAL EXPRESSION AFTER LEAVING MOM...

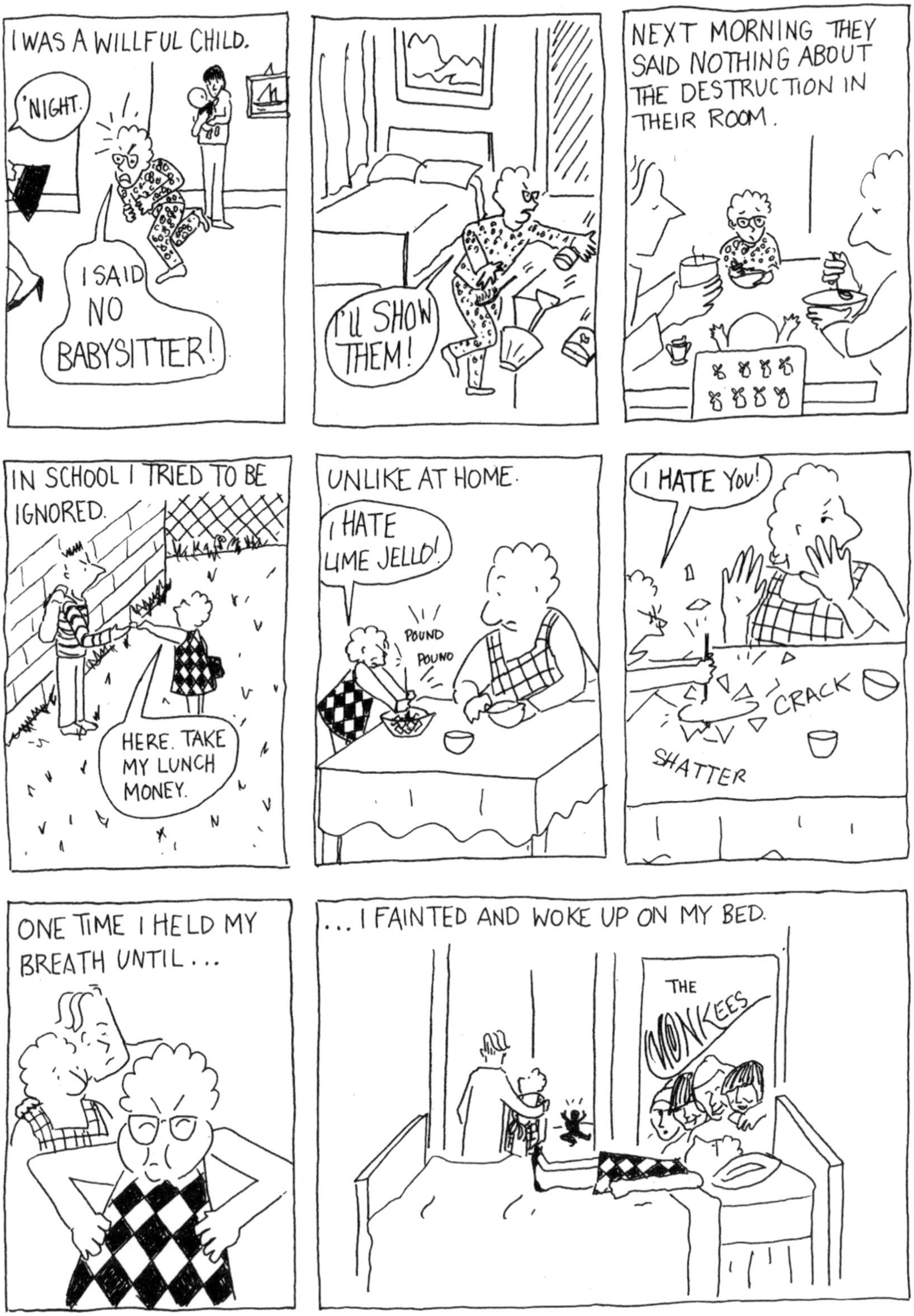
I WAS A WILLFUL CHILD.
'NIGHT.
I SAID NO BABYSITTER!
I'LL SHOW THEM!
NEXT MORNING THEY SAID NOTHING ABOUT THE DESTRUCTION IN THEIR ROOM.
IN SCHOOL I TRIED TO BE IGNORED.
HERE. TAKE MY LUNCH MONEY.
UNLIKE AT HOME.
I HATE LIME JELLO!
POUND
POUND
I HATE YOU!
CRACK
SHATTER
ONE TIME I HELD MY BREATH UNTIL...
...I FAINTED AND WOKE UP ON MY BED.
THE MONKEES

LET'S JUST LET HER REST.

THE MONKEES

SHHHH NOW.

THERE, THERE. IT'S OK.

THE MONKEES

ANOTHER TIME, WHEN I WAS A TEENAGER, I HAD A FIERCE TANTRUM.

NO! NO! NO! NO! NO! NO! NO! NO! NO!

I DON'T REMEMBER WHAT IT WAS ABOUT...

... BUT I REMEMBER DAD SLAPPED ME ACROSS MY FACE.

FINALLY! ATTENTION!

MY TANTRUMS ALWAYS HAPPENED IN OCTOBER JUST AFTER SCHOOL STARTED.

EVEN THOUGH EACH PARENT-TEACHER NIGHT...

SHE'S AN EXCELLENT STUDENT. VERY QUIET. STRAIGHT A's.

... I KNEW MOM FOUND ME JUST WRONG, BUT...

YEAH, BUT SHE'S WEIRD, ISN'T SHE?

I'LL KEEP THAT TO MYSELF.

STIFF UPPER LIP →

MOM BLAMED HERSELF.

I ONLY EVER WANTED TO BE A WIFE AND MOTHER.

BUT I THINK I WAS BETTER AT MY PAID JOB.

I DIDN'T KNOW WHAT SHE MEANT BUT I SENSED THIS WAS MY FAULT.

AHHHH

IT'S ALL RIGHT. SIGH.

CERTAINLY I WAS WRONG FOR PIANO LESSONS.

I'VE NEVER HAD A STUDENT WITH LESS RHYTHM!

ONE! TWO! THREE!

WHACK! WHACK! WHACK!

I LOVED TO DRAW. I WANTED TO BE A DRESS DESIGNER.

MOM SEEMED ALMOST HAPPY WHEN I FAILED SEWING IN JUNIOR HIGH.

YOU'LL NEVER BE A DRESS DESIGNER IF YOU CAN'T SEW.

I GOT THE MESSAGE THAT MOM FOUND ME A LOT OF TROUBLE.

I WOULD HATE IT IF YOU DIED AT AGE 16. ALL THAT WORK—FOR NOTHING!

LOVE?

MOM HAD A LOT OF SHOULDS.

RED AND GREEN SHOULD NEVER BE SEEN.

YOU SHOULD ONLY BE A NURSE, SECRETARY, OR TEACHER.

YOU'LL NEVER GET A JOB AS AN ARTIST.

I'VE JUST SIGNED YOU UP FOR CHURCH CHOIR.

GREAT. I HATE CHURCH AND I'M ROTTEN AT MUSIC.

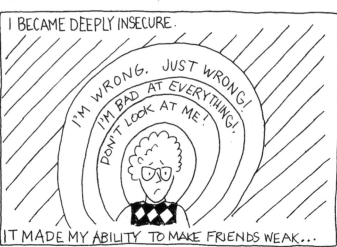

I BECAME DEEPLY INSECURE.

I'M WRONG. JUST WRONG!

I'M BAD AT EVERYTHING!

DON'T LOOK AT ME!

IT MADE MY ABILITY TO MAKE FRIENDS WEAK...

...AND MY ABILITY TO HATE MY BROTHER GREW STRONG. I THINK THAT'S WHEN YOU COULD START CALLING ME A WOUNDED CHILD.

IT'S HIS FAULT SOMEHOW!

STUPID BROTHER!

EVEN AS AN ADULT I MADE THAT CLEAR TO HIM.

WHAT DOES FAIS DODO MEAN IN THIS KIDS' SONG?

HMMMM I DON'T KNOW.

OHHHHH? I THOUGHT YOU LEARNED FRENCH THE YEAR YOU SPENT IN FRANCE.

IT FELT VISCERALLY SATISFYING TO MAKE HIM WRONG.

HONESTLY? DID THEY NEED TO GIVE BIRTH TO HIM?

MY FATHER WAS A WORRIER. ONCE WHEN I WAS IN UNIVERSITY...

DON'T DRIVE HOME THIS WEEKEND!

THEY'RE PREDICTING FLURRIES!

LATER IN LIFE DAD CAME INTO MONEY THROUGH A VETERANS' PENSION HE DIDN'T KNOW ABOUT.

WHY DIDN'T ANYONE TELL ME?

Canada

MOM WANTED TO TRAVEL WITH THE MONEY AND DAD SOMETIMES WENT WITH HER.

BUT OFTEN...

I'M NOT FLYING!

TWA CRASH!

FIND YOURSELF ANOTHER FOOL!

MOM HAD LONG SEEN DAD AS WEAK AND FEARFUL.

YOUR FATHER ACTUALLY SPENT WORLD WAR II IN A SANATORIUM IN BED WITH TB.

I THINK HE GOT TB BECAUSE HE WAS TOO SCARED TO GO OVERSEAS.

MOM WAS BIG ON BLAME.

MY FATHER HAD THREE BROTHERS AND TWO SISTERS.

MacLEODS ARE LAZY!

I'M A MacLEOD. AM I LAZY?

BUT SHE WAS ONLY TALKING ABOUT THE MEN.

SISTERS-IN-LAWS AT A PICNIC...

HAVE YOU EVER NOTICED HOW MacLEOD MEN MARRIED STRONG CAPABLE WOMEN WHO TAKE ON ALL THE FAMILY AND OTHER RESPONSIBILITIES?

YUP.

OH YEAH.

THEY RUN A MILE FROM RESPONSIBILITY.

DAD WAS A POPULAR RACONTEUR.

AND THEN THEY BEGAN SHOOTING AT THE GATORS!

I TURNED FOR A SECOND TO BUY POP AND THE KNOCK-OUT HAPPENED!

I MISSED THE WHOLE THING!

AND AFTER WE DROVE ACROSS THE BORDER INTO FLORIDA, THE OLD GALS IN THE BACK TOOK OFF THEIR TOPS AND STARTED WHOOPING!

MOM'S STORIES WERE ALWAYS PAINFUL.

DAD TOLD ME ABOUT MY PERIOD BECAUSE MY MOTHER JUST REFUSED TO.

MOM WOULD STOP SPEAKING TO US FOR WEEKS ON END. WE DIDN'T KNOW WHY.

MY FATHER WAS VERY PASSIVE. HE DIDN'T STAND UP TO HER.

DESPITE HER INTELLIGENCE, MOM DID POORLY IN SCHOOL. MAYBE SHE WAS DEPRESSED. HER HOME LIFE WAS UNHAPPY.

AT AGE 16, QUEENIE, AS HER MOTHER WAS KNOWN, SENT MOM TO BE A MAID FAR AWAY.

I WAS A SLAVE THERE.

WHEN I WAS FOUR, MOM'S DAD HAD A STROKE. I THOUGHT IT WAS VERY STRANGE TO SEE HIM IN A BED IN QUEENIE'S LIVING ROOM.

PAPA?

WTF?!

WHEN I WAS AN ADULT, DAD RECOUNTED THAT HE AND MOM WERE ANXIOUS ABOUT LEAVING PAPA ALONE WITH QUEENIE. THEY WERE AFRAID SHE WOULD HURT HIM. I WAS TOO STUNNED TO ASK MORE.

WTF?!

QUEENIE SPENT HER LAST DAYS IN A NURSING HOME.

WELCOME.

QUEENIE'S NURSING HOME WAS TWO HOURS AWAY. MOM LOATHED VISITING HER AND ONLY DID SO THREE TIMES A YEAR.

QUEENIE DIED WHEN I WAS IN UNIVERSITY. MOM CALLED TO TELL ME.

I NEVER CARED FOR HER MUCH. I DON'T KNOW WHY I'M UPSET.

WELL, SHE WAS YOUR MOTHER.

YES... SHE WAS.

MOM HAD *NEITHER* A GOOD ROLE MODEL IN HER PARENTS...

YOUR MOTHER SEEMS TO HAVE STOPPED SPEAKING TO US AGAIN.

...NOR MUCH SUPPORT IN HER MARRIAGE.

LET'S TALK ABOUT SUSAN'S TANTRUMS.

DAD'S ONLY REAL HOUSE-HOLD ROLE WAS VETO POWER.

NO!

WE NEED A NEW LIVING ROOM LAMP.

SO MY BROTHER AND I WERE LOVED IN A WAY, BUT WITH LITTLE EMOTIONAL UNDERSTANDING OR SUPPORT.

HERE'S EVERYTHING WE NEVER HAD.

I WANT ART LESSONS!

PIANO LESSONS

UNIVERSITY SAVINGS

SCHOOL SUPPLIES

CHURCH CAMPS AND CHOIR

AND THEN THERE WAS ME. I DON'T KNOW MY BROTHER'S EXPERIENCE WITH MOM AND DAD, BUT I KNOW SOMETHING ABOUT HIS EXPERIENCE WITH ME.

WHY DON'T YOU EVER OFFER TO CLEAR THE TABLE?!

46

THE YEAR MY BROTHER WENT BACKPACKING IN FRANCE, HE DIDN'T KEEP IN TOUCH.

I HOPE HE'S NOT SICK.

I HOPE HE DIDN'T GET KIDNAPPED AND SOLD INTO A SLAVE TRADE!

NO INTERNET BACK THEN. I TOOK COMMUNICATING INTO MY OWN HANDS.

YOU KNOW HOW MUCH THEY WORRY! SEND THEM A POSTCARD!!

HE DIDN'T. WHEN HE RETURNED HE GAVE THE FAMILY A SLIDESHOW OF HIS TRAVEL PHOTOS. I WALKED OUT. HE AND I HAD LITTLE TO DO WITH EACH OTHER AFTER THAT.

BORING

A META MOMENT. WHILE I'M WRITING THIS, I HAVE NIGHTMARES OF A LITTLE BOY CRYING WILDLY AND LOOKING FOR ME.

I TRY TALKING TO HIM SENSIBLY. BUT I WON'T HUG HIM.

SOON AFTER, MY BROTHER MOVED FAR AWAY. I IMAGINE LIVING FAR AWAY FELT SAFE FOR HIM.

A YEAR AFTER DAD DIED, MOM WAS FINALLY ABLE TO START THE PROCESS FOR ASSISTED LIVING.

YOUR APPOINTMENT WITH DR. DODGE IS 2PM TUESDAY.

SHE PASSED THE COGNITIVE TEST WITH FLYING COLOURS.

WHO'S THE PRIME MINISTER?

HARPER!

WE FOUND A PLACE NOT FAR FROM WHERE SHE LIVED.

MY FAMILY MOVED HER AND GOT RID OF SURPLUS THINGS. IT WAS EXPENSIVE BUT WORTH IT. SHE STILL HAD DAD'S VETERANS' PENSION.

YOU OK, GRANDMA?

OH YES!

IT SEEMED LIKE SUCH A RELIEF FOR ALL OF US.

WELCOME TO YOUR NEW HOME

MEALS, MEDICAL STAFF, FUN!

MOM SEEMED CONTENT TO BE WITHOUT DAD.

NOW, THIS IS THE WAY I LIKE A ROOM!

I REMEMBER BEFORE MY FATHER DIED, MY BROTHER HAPPENED TO BE VISITING FOR A FEW WEEKS.

BEFORE HE FLEW BACK, HE TOOK A DAY TRIP TO THE PLACE WE GREW UP, 100 MILES AWAY.

HE GOT WAYLAID AND, NOT HAVING A PHONE, DIDN'T CALL TO SAY HE'D BE LATE.

AHHHH. MY BELOVED OCEAN.

AGAIN, TRUE TO FORM...

I HOPE HE DIDN'T GET A FLAT TIRE.

I HOPE HE DIDN'T GET KIDNAPPED AND SOLD INTO SLAVERY OR DIE IN A FIERY CRASH!!

MOM BELIEVED THE ANXIETY HE SUFFERED THAT DAY LED TO HIS HEART ATTACK AND DEATH DAYS LATER. (BIG ON BLAME.)

JUST ONE CALL...

IT'S HIGHLY UNLIKELY DAD'S DEATH WAS CAUSED BY MY BROTHER.

MR. BROTHER IN THE LIVING ROOM WITH THE SILENT PHONE.

MOM, HE WAS 88, HAD A BAD HEART CONDITION, PROSTATE CANCER AND HIGH ANXIETY.

BUT A DEATH CAN BRING OUT THE WORST.

AND TELL ME MORE ABOUT THE WAYS YOUR SON IS UTTERLY THOUGHTLESS.

AND SO MY BROTHER AND I WERE WELL-POISED TO BE ADVERSARIAL AS OUR MOTHER DECLINED.

SHE'S YOUR MOTHER TOO!

MEANWHILE, MOM'S BLISS IN HER NEW HOME WAS TURNING INTO BILE.

CHAPTER FOUR

THE RIGHT CARE AT THE RIGHT TIME IN THE RIGHT PLACE.

RIGHT.

FINDING FLAWS IN HER NEW ASSISTED LIVING PLACE, MOM QUICKLY TOOK MATTERS INTO HER OWN HANDS.

WTF!?

HAPPY ST. PATRICK'S DAY!

I INSIST YOU HANG THIS FOR ST. GEORGE'S DAY!

MOM HAD AN AMERICAN TABLE MATE.

THE ROYAL FAMILY ARE WEALTHY LEECHES!

YOU IGNORANT VIPER!

SHE WASN'T HAPPY WITH THE STAFF EITHER.

IN MY DAY, WE WORE PROPER UNIFORMS. WHITE! STARCHED!

IN BOX

I AGREED WITH HER CONCERNS ABOUT THE NIGHT STAFFING.

IF I FALL IN THE BATHROOM IN THE NIGHT AND RING THE BELL, ONLY SECURITY MEN COME!

AND THEN THEY CALL AN AMBULANCE EVEN IF I JUST NEED HELP GETTING BACK ON MY FEET.

NO ONE ELSE WAS ON STAFF AT NIGHT.

MOM DIDN'T ENDEAR HERSELF TO ANYONE.

THEY'RE ALL OVERWEIGHT!

AND WHO'S THAT ONE CALLING?

MOM!

THE PHILIPPINES!?

I BLAME UNIONS!

AT HER INSISTENCE, MY FAMILY MOVED HER TO A NON-UNION ASSISTED LIVING HOME.

THERE WAS STILL LOTS TO GET RID OF.

MOVING WAS A LOT OF WORK, PHYSICALLY AND EMOTIONALLY, ON TOP OF OUR BUSY LIVES.

I KEPT MY BROTHER INFORMED AND GOT BRIEF REPLIES, NO EMPATHY, NO CONCERN.

I THREW OUT THE WINE BOTTLE LAMP MOM MADE. KINDA SAD.

TAP TAP

OK. THANKS.

WHAT WAS I EXPECTING?

I BEGAN TO FEEL A LONGING FOR SOMEONE WHO ALSO KNEW MOM FOR A LONG TIME, SOMEONE WHO COULD SHARE THE LOSS AND DREAD I FELT.

HEY! LOOK OVER HERE!

NO.

MOM LOVED HER NEW SPACE BUT THE HOME DIDN'T HAVE A DOCTOR.

LOOK AT THE BIRDS! THIS IS MY AERIE!

WHEN PHYSICIANS NEGOTIATED THEIR GOVERNMENT CONTRACT THEY AGREED TO LESS PAY FOR LONG-TERM CARE VISITS.

SO, WE NEGLECT THE FRAIL ELDERLY THEN?

DEAL!

THAT MEANT MANY DOCS WOULDN'T GO TO CARE HOMES AT ALL. I WORKED IN HEALTH CARE. LUCKY ME.

MY MOTHER IS 93 AND DOESN'T HAVE A DOCTOR.

DR. MAJOR EXEC. DIRECTOR

WELL, SHE CAN BE MY PATIENT BUT I'LL PUT HER UNDER THE CARE OF A GERIATRIC NURSE PRACTITIONER.

I THANK YOU. I THANK YOU. I WORSHIP YOU.

DR. MAJOR EXEC. DIRECTOR

I NOTICED MOM WAS SLOWING DOWN ON OUR WALKS.

I THINK HERE IS FAR ENOUGH.

LET'S GO BACK AND REST.

ONE TIME, SHE SAID QUITE SERIOUSLY....

WELL, SINCE YOU'RE MY **MOTHER**, YOU SHOULD KNOW.

THE WORKERS AT THE HOME EXPLAINED HOW THEY CHANGED HER MEDS.

WE'RE UPPING HER $\text{2H} \wedge \Sigma \ominus e = \sum$ AND ADDING $e\Sigma \ominus\angle IIIM$ FOR HER DEMENTIA.

GOTTA GO.

ONE DAY MOM AND I WENT OUT FOR A FEW GROCERIES. I GOT DISTRACTED.

HI! NICE TO SEE YOU!

OH HI!

MA'AM! MA'AM!

MOM WAS NO LONGER UP FOR SHOPPING

I'M SO SORRY, MOM.

I TOOK THAT ON.

I WANT YOU TO KNOW THESE ARE NOT FOR ME.

OH?

DEPENDS DEPENDS DEPENDS DEPENDS DEPENDS

I FOUND THE BURDEN INCREASINGLY DIFFICULT TO MANAGE.

HMMMM... WHERE CAN I FIND HELP TO UNDERSTAND WHAT I'M GOING THROUGH— AFFORDABLE, ACCESSIBLE, UNDERSTANDABLE HELP?

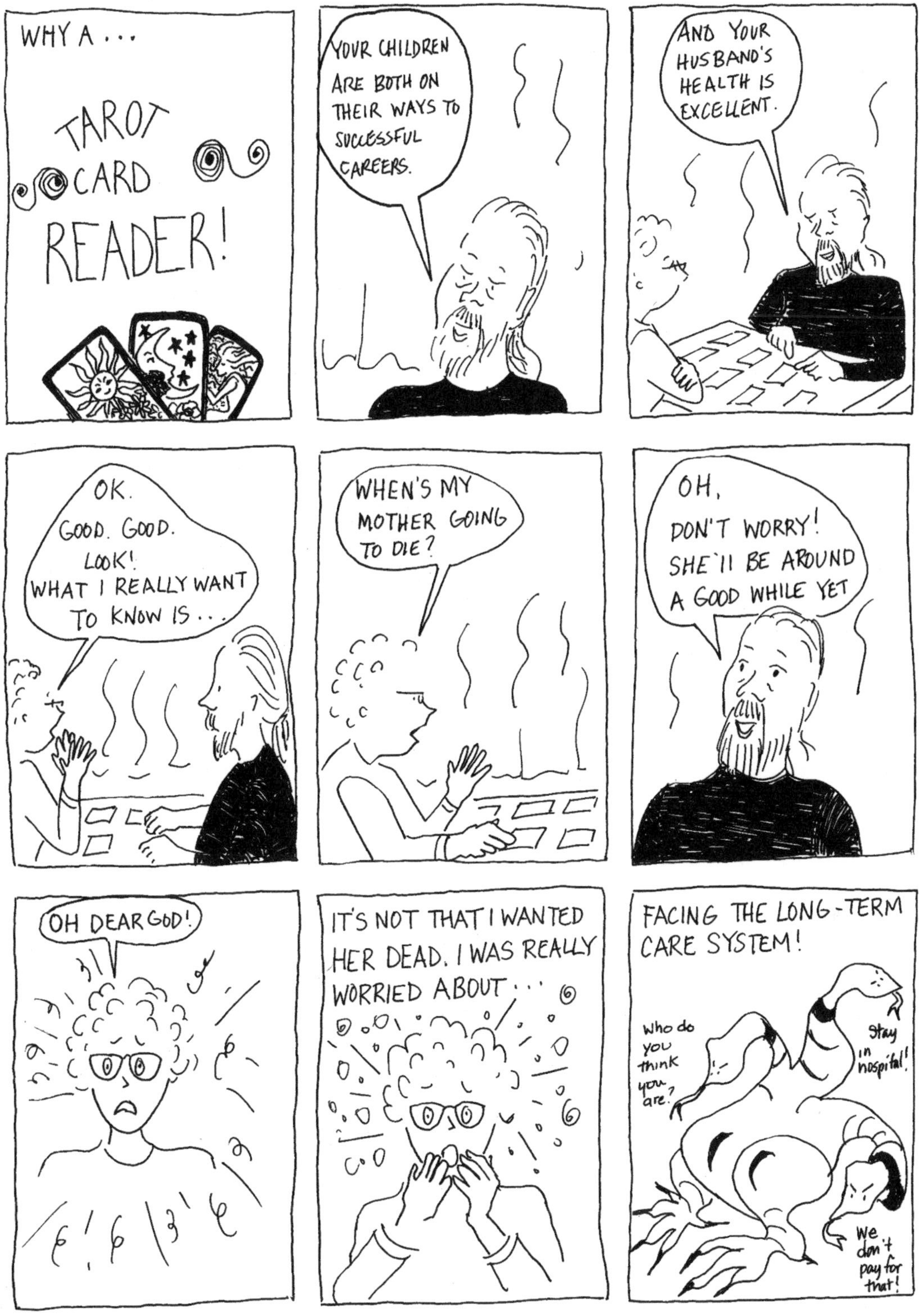
WHY A . . .
TAROT CARD READER!
YOUR CHILDREN ARE BOTH ON THEIR WAYS TO SUCCESSFUL CAREERS.
AND YOUR HUSBAND'S HEALTH IS EXCELLENT.
OK. GOOD. GOOD. LOOK! WHAT I REALLY WANT TO KNOW IS . . .
WHEN'S MY MOTHER GOING TO DIE?
OH, DON'T WORRY! SHE'LL BE AROUND A GOOD WHILE YET
OH DEAR GOD!
IT'S NOT THAT I WANTED HER DEAD. I WAS REALLY WORRIED ABOUT . . .
FACING THE LONG-TERM CARE SYSTEM!
Who do you think you are?
Stay in hospital!
We don't pay for that!

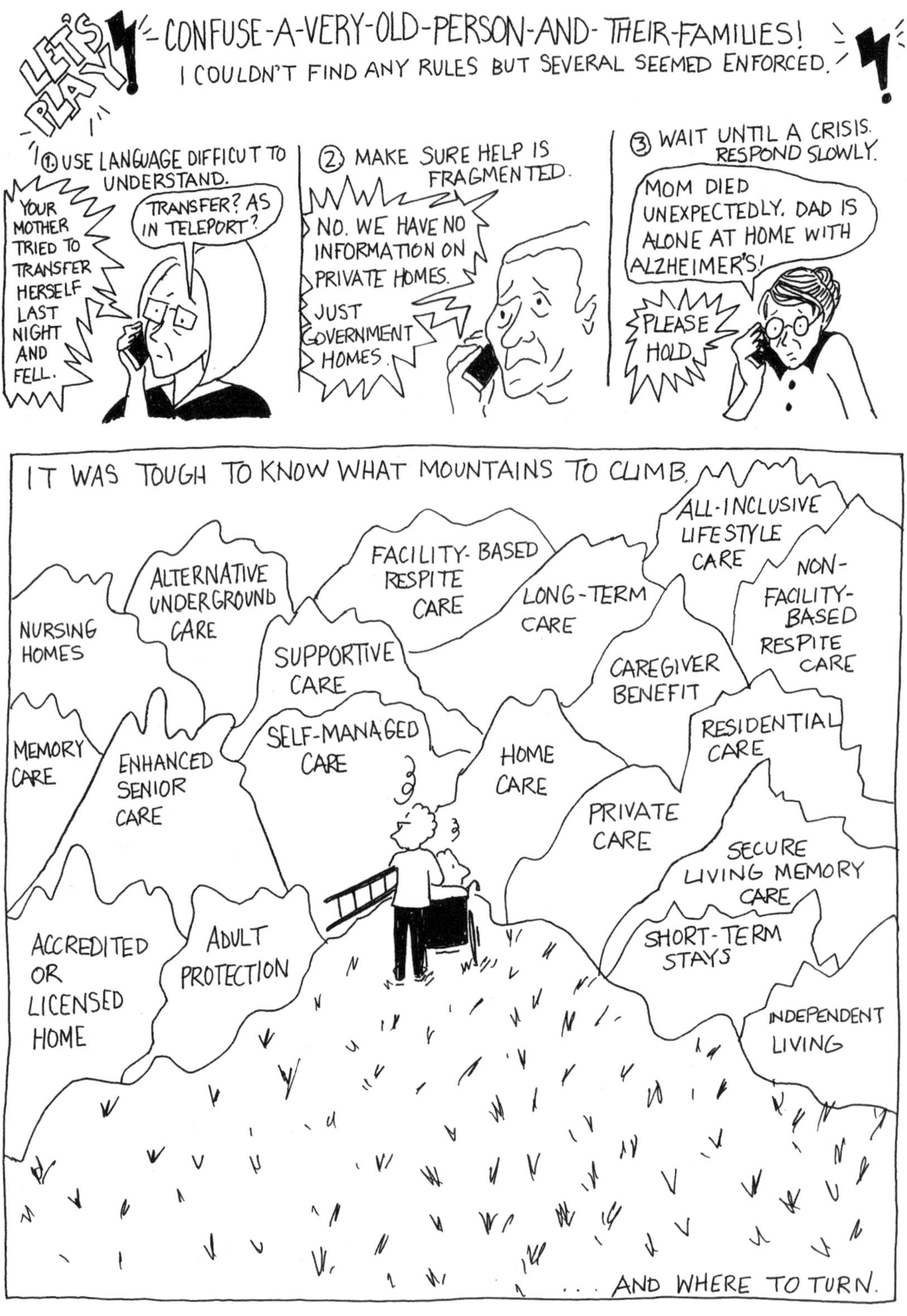
LET'S PLAY!
CONFUSE-A-VERY-OLD-PERSON-AND-THEIR-FAMILIES!
I COULDN'T FIND ANY RULES BUT SEVERAL SEEMED ENFORCED.
1. USE LANGUAGE DIFFICUT TO UNDERSTAND.
YOUR MOTHER TRIED TO TRANSFER HERSELF LAST NIGHT AND FELL.
TRANSFER? AS IN TELEPORT?
2. MAKE SURE HELP IS FRAGMENTED.
NO. WE HAVE NO INFORMATION ON PRIVATE HOMES.
JUST GOVERNMENT HOMES.
3. WAIT UNTIL A CRISIS. RESPOND SLOWLY.
MOM DIED UNEXPECTEDLY. DAD IS ALONE AT HOME WITH ALZHEIMER'S!
PLEASE HOLD
IT WAS TOUGH TO KNOW WHAT MOUNTAINS TO CLIMB.
NURSING HOMES
ALTERNATIVE UNDERGROUND CARE
FACILITY-BASED RESPITE CARE
LONG-TERM CARE
ALL-INCLUSIVE LIFESTYLE CARE
NON-FACILITY-BASED RESPITE CARE
SUPPORTIVE CARE
CAREGIVER BENEFIT
MEMORY CARE
ENHANCED SENIOR CARE
SELF-MANAGED CARE
HOME CARE
RESIDENTIAL CARE
PRIVATE CARE
SECURE LIVING MEMORY CARE
SHORT-TERM STAYS
ACCREDITED OR LICENSED HOME
ADULT PROTECTION
INDEPENDENT LIVING
. . . AND WHERE TO TURN.

AT THE BEGINNING OF MY COMMUNICATIONS CAREER I WAS PRETTY BAD AT IT.

THIS IS POORLY WRITTEN.

AND FULL OF TYPOS!

BUT MOST OF THE LETTERS ARE RIGHT, AREN'T THEY?

I HAD PROMOTED A THEATRE GROUP AND MY PUBLIC RELATIONS AGENCY ASKED ME TO ATTEND A PLAY AND MEET THE ACTORS BACKSTAGE.

I WAS TOO SHY TO DO THAT. I THOUGHT I WASN'T GOOD ENOUGH TO MEET **REAL LIVE** ACTORS.

THEATRE

THE ONLY POSITIVE THING ON MY PERFORMANCE REVIEW WAS THAT I DRESSED PROFESSIONALLY.

HMMM. I'M NOT KNOWN FOR MY FASHION SENSE.

I WAS IN MY EARLY 20's, RIGHT OUT OF UNIVERSITY. MOM BEGAN TO CONFIDE IN ME AS IF I WAS AN ADULT.

I'M NOT HAPPY IN OUR MARRIAGE ANY MORE.

I WASN'T AN ADULT.

FOR ONE THING, HE DOESN'T WANT TO HAVE SEX.

SOMETIME AROUND THEN, DAD STARTED GROPING ME, QUICKLY, WHEN OTHER PEOPLE WERE AROUND.

I FELT STUNNED AND PARALYZED.

I DIDN'T SAY ANYTHING BUT THE DISTANCE BETWEEN US GREW.

ONCE, MOM HAD A NON LIFE-THREATENING SURGERY.

IF SHE DIES, WHO'S GOING TO LOOK AFTER THE COOKING, THE LAUNDRY, THE BILLS? ME?!?

NOT ME! FIND YOURSELF ANOTHER FOOL!

DESPITE SUCH POOR COMMUNICATIONS AT HOME, I GOT BETTER AT MY JOB OVER TIME.

WELL DONE!

WANG

I WON MINOR AWARDS...

HONORABLE MENTION

CORPORATE NEWSLETTER CATEGORY

NATIONAL PR ASSOCIATION

...AND LEARNED HOW TO BE INTERVIEWED.

CONGRATULATIONS! YOU BEAT OUT 60 OTHER APPLICANTS FOR THIS JOB!

SHE REALLY IS EXCEPTIONAL. I BELIEVE SHE COULD CURRENTLY DO THE JOB OF COMMUNICATIONS DIRECTOR FOR THE DEPARTMENT OF HEALTH.

I OVERHEARD THIS.

I HAD TWO REACTIONS.

WOW! MONEY!

IMPOSTER!

I WAS NAIVE.

I HAVE A SUGGESTION. WHY DON'T GOVERNMENT HEALTH BUREAUCRATS VOLUNTEER ONCE A MONTH AT THE INSTITUTIONS THEY'RE FUNDING?

THAT WOULD HELP THEM MAKE INFORMED DECISIONS.

OFFICE OF THE DEPUTY MINISTER

HA HA HA
HAHA
HAHA

I HAD THE CONTINUING CARE FILE. I DIDN'T HAVE A CLUE WHAT IT WAS.

WHY WOULD CARE NEED TO CONTINUE?

YOUNG. NAIVE.

I DEVELOPED A BROCHURE WITH ALL THE DETAILS.

CONTINUING CARE, OR LONG TERM CARE, IS PROVIDED TO ELIGIBLE PEOPLE WHO NEED CARE OUTSIDE HOSPITAL.

GOOD READING.

I INCLUDED THE FACT THAT WAIT TIMES FOR CARE HOMES COULD BE SIX MONTHS OR LONGER.

BEST PEOPLE KNOW.

DURING QUESTION PERIOD, THE OPPOSITION PARTY ATTACKED THE GOVERNMENT FOR THIS SENTENCE.

ARE YOU SAYING PEOPLE HAVE TO STAY IN HOSPITAL FOR ALMOST A YEAR BEFORE YOU'RE GOING TO HELP THEM?!

THE MEDIA JOINED THE ATTACK AND MY BOSSES WERE FURIOUS.

ARE YOU TRYING TO BRING DOWN THE GOVERNMENT?

WHAT WERE YOU THINKING?

!

UMM, I WAS BEING OPEN AND TRANSPARENT?

THE MINISTER OF HEALTH WAS A GOOD MAN.

WE ALWAYS TRY TO BE OPEN AND TRANSPARENT.

RIGHT.

DESPITE THAT GOOF-UP, I REMAINED COMMITTED TO GOVERNMENT MESSAGING.

OK.

RIGHT CARE.
RIGHT TIME.
RIGHT PLACE.

RIGHT CARE.
RIGHT TIME.
RIGHT PLACE.

RIGHT CARE.
RIGHT TIME.
RIGHT PLACE.

GOT IT!

FOR THE ANNUAL SENIORS' EXPOSITION, I ORDERED A LARGE BOOTH DISPLAY.

CONTINUING CARE
RIGHT CARE
RIGHT TIME
RIGHT PLACE
GOVERNMENT IN ACTION!
HERE FOR YOU

I DID A SHIFT STAFFING IT. ENTHUSIASTICALLY!

STEP RIGHT UP!

YES! WE PROVIDE THE RIGHT CARE AT THE RIGHT TIME IN THE RIGHT PLACE!

I BELIEVED IT!

UNTIL...

HEY! TAKE A FREE BROCHURE!

CONTINUING

HEY! I GET THE WRONG CARE, THERE'S NEVER ENOUGH TIME FOR ME AND THERE'S NO RIGHT PLACE.

I'M PUT ON GERIATRIC UNITS!

I'M 39!

CONTINUING CARE
RIGHT CARE
RIGHT TIME
RIGHT PLA

GOVERNMENT ACTION!
YOU

I WANTED THE FLOOR TO SWALLOW ME.

MEANWHILE, MOM WAS ALSO SINKING.

AND I WAS COMING FACE-TO-FACE WITH WHAT

LONG-TERM CARE

REALLY MEANS.

MY BOOTH DISPLAY WAS FOR
THE BIRDS.

CHAPTER FIVE

DECODING ELDER-MARKETING

WHAT'S REALLY BEING SOLD

SPRINT SCOOTER

DELUXE COMMODE

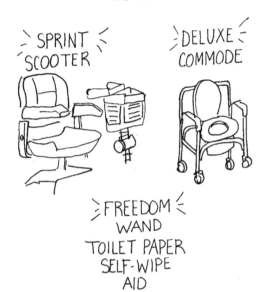

FREEDOM WAND
TOILET PAPER
SELF-WIPE
AID

OVER CHRISTMAS, MOM SEEMED TENSE AND QUIET AT HER NEW ASSISTED LIVING HOME.

MOM, HERE'S YOUR SHERRY. MOM?

SHE WOULDN'T EVEN WATCH HER BELOVED ALASTAIR SIM'S "A CHRISTMAS CAROL."

BUT MOM, THE GHOSTS HAVEN'T HAUNTED YET.

THIS HOME WAS STAFFED WITH ONE LICENSED PRACTICAL NURSE (LPN) AND SEVERAL CONTINUING CARE WORKERS. NO RN.

YOUR MOM'S FINE.

I ARRANGED FOR THE GERIATRIC NURSE PRACTITIONER TO SEE MOM THE FIRST WORK DAY IN JANUARY.

PLEASE?

AT 10:00AM SHE CALLED ME.

SUSAN, COME RIGHT AWAY! I'M SENDING HER TO HOSPITAL!

I NOW KNOW THAT THE ELDERLY WITH PAIN HAVE DIFFICULTY COMMUNICATING THAT.

HOW DOES PAIN AFFECT PEOPLE WITH DEMENTIA? — ALZHEIMER SOCIETY —

AS A PERSON'S DEMENTIA PROGRESSES, HIS OR HER LANGUAGE SKILLS MAY CHANGE MAKING IT VERY DIFFICULT TO COMMUNICATE WHEN THEY ARE IN PAIN.

I WASN'T THE ONLY ONE IN THE DARK THEN. AS MOM WAS LEAVING FOR THE HOSPITAL,...

SUSAN! SUSAN!

AMBULANC

WHY DID THE NURSE PRACTITIONER SEND HER TO HOSPITAL?

SHE'S IN A GREAT DEAL OF PAIN.

WHY COULDN'T YOU SEE THAT?

PARAME

AT THE HOSPITAL, WE WERE WELCOMED BY THE CHARGE NURSE.

AND JUST WHO IS THIS?!?

GERIATRIC UNIT

SHE HADN'T RECEIVED A MESSAGE

AND WHO TEACHES NURSES TO TALK TO PARAMEDICS THAT WAY?

MOM DETERIORATED IN HOSPITAL. SHE TRIED TO SCRATCH STAFF.

THE NURSE MANAGER TOOK ME INTO A SUPPLY CLOSET TO SPEAK TO ME PRIVATELY.

SHE'S SAYING SOME REALLY VULGAR THINGS!

WHAT?!

BY THIS TIME, I WAS EMPLOYED IN COMMUNICATIONS AT THE HOSPITAL. I KNEW THIS MANAGER.

HAS SHE ALWAYS BEEN LIKE THIS?

NO!

HOW MORTIFYING!

MOM WAS DIFFICULT BUT I CAN'T SAY THE STAFF ON THE UNIT WERE OVERLY IMBUED WITH THE MILK OF HUMAN KINDNESS.

SHE INSISTS ON GOING TO BED AT 6:30 P.M. THEN SHE WAKES UP AT 10:00 P.M. AND RINGS HER BELL ALL NIGHT!

SHE WAS COMPLAINING ABOUT MOM IN THE HALLWAY!

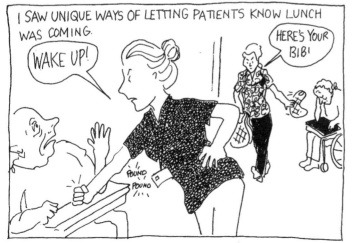

I SAW UNIQUE WAYS OF LETTING PATIENTS KNOW LUNCH WAS COMING.

WAKE UP!

POUND POUND

HERE'S YOUR BIB!

THE FEW KIND NURSES AND THE OVERWROUGHT ONES SEEMED TO IGNORE EACH OTHER.

YOUR BIB!

LET ME HELP YOU.

MOM STAYED IN HOSPITAL TWO WEEKS. SOMETHING WAS WRONG WITH HER LEFT-BACK-HIP AREA.

THE DOCTORS COULDN'T SAY WHAT.

IT WAS DECIDED SHE NEEDED 24/7 NURSING HOME CARE. AND LOTS OF PAIN MEDS.

SHE CAN'T GO HOME

NO DIAGNOSTIC SURGERY AT 92.

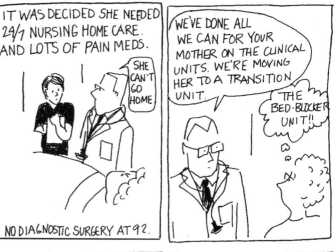

WE'VE DONE ALL WE CAN FOR YOUR MOTHER ON THE CLINICAL UNITS. WE'RE MOVING HER TO A TRANSITION UNIT.

THE BED-BLOCKER UNIT!!

HOW LONG WILL SHE STAY THERE?

AT LEAST SIX MONTHS.

WHAT?!

OH NOOOOO

I KNEW THE ELDERLY WERE PRONE TO INFECTIONS DURING LONG HOSPITAL STAYS.

MS. MACLEOD? I'M MARIE, THE SOCIAL WORKER.

COME TO MY OFFICE AND I'LL TELL YOU ABOUT GETTING A NURSING HOME BED.

SHE PROCEEDED.

HERE'S A LIST OF NURSING HOMES WITHIN A 70 MILE RADIUS. PICK YOUR TOP THREE. WHEN YOUR MOTHER'S NAME COMES UP YOU HAVE TO TAKE IT OR GO TO THE BOTTOM OF THE LIST. YOU ALREADY HAVE POWER OF ATTORNEY. OTHERWISE SHE'LL PROBABLY STAY IN HOSPITAL FOR SIX MONTHS.

I HEARD: BLAH BLAH BLAH BLAH BLAH BLAH BLAH BLAH BLAH BLAH BLAH BLAH BLAH BLAH BLAH BLAH BLAH BLAH BLAH

AH, HUH? WHY DOES SHE NEED 24/7 CARE AGAIN?

THE DOCTOR TOLD YOU THAT.

dummy

HOW DO I KNOW WHICH OF THESE HOMES GIVE THE BEST CARE?

I'M NOT ALLOWED TO COMMENT ON THAT.

WHAT MATTERS TO ME.

THAT HORRIBLE SINKING FEELING. I KNOW FROM MY GOVERNMENT WORK THERE ARE HOMES WITH FREQUENT INFRACTIONS! BUT WHICH ONES? HELP! MOM! I'M SCARED! I DREW THIS. HOW I NOTICE AS I DRAW THIS HOW VERY CLAUSTROPHOBIC MY WORK IS BECOMING. I'M EVEN DIZZY!

IN THE TRANSITION UNIT, MOM GOT WORSE. SHE HAD AN INFECTION.

I DROPPED BY AFTER WORK TO FIND HER VERY ILL AND REFUSING TO EAT. I SPENT THE EVENING WITH HER.

MOM, ANOTHER ONE.

JUST ONE MORE.

YOU'RE GOING TO BE FINE MOM. JUST ONE MORE.

NOOOOOOooo

FINALLY SHE STABILIZED.

IT'S GREAT YOU'RE PART OF THE TEAM.

NO STAFF HAD TIME TO PATIENTLY FEED HER.

MOM RETURNED TO HER NORMAL SELF.

FURTHERMORE, THE FOOD IS BAD, YOU GIVE ME TOO MANY PILLS AND THE HALLWAYS ARE NOISY!

THE RESIDENT SNAPPED.

WE ALL DO THE BEST WE CAN! YOU'RE LUCKY! YOU ALMOST DIED!

PFFT.

PART OF ME DIDN'T BLAME HIM.

MY DAUGHTER HAD A SUMMER JOB NEARBY AND VISITED EACH MORNING.

Hi GRANDMA!

MY HUSBAND AND SON VISITED AS WORK ALLOWED.

I KEPT MY BROTHER INFORMED IN DETAIL...

OK. THANKS.

WE HAVE TO PICK THREE HOMES. I HAVE NO IDEA HOW...

...AND RECEIVED UNDETAILED REPLIES.

THERE WAS ONE HOSPITAL EXPERIENCE I WON'T FORGET. I DREW THIS EXAMPLE OF SHITTY COMMUNICATIONS AFTER RETURNING HOME ONE DAY.

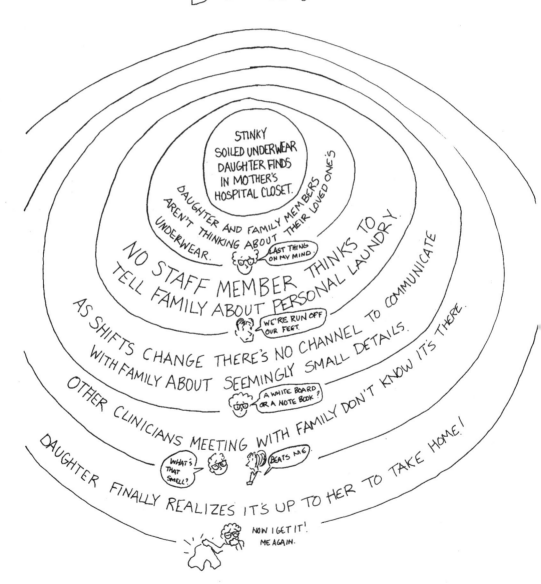

THERE WAS ALWAYS SHITTY NEWS ABOUT HEALTH CARE.

DAILY NEWS

ANOTHER HEALTH CARE CRISIS

THIS AFTERNOON POLITICIANS RELUCTANT TO MAKE DIFFICULT DECISIONS FOR LONG-TERM SYSTEM SUSTAINABILITY AND COMPASSION.

I WANT MORE FOR ME

PHYSICIANS AND NURSES CLASH IN STREET
SURGEONS CURSE ADMINISTRATORS

THE CEO OF OUR HOSPITAL DISTRICT TOOK MATTERS INTO HER OWN HANDS.

SOMEONE'S GOT TO DO SOMETHING DIFFERENT!

WE'LL DO IT!

THE PREMISE WAS THAT NOTHING WILL CHANGE UNLESS WE EACH CHANGE.

HOW MIGHT I RESPOND DIFFERENTLY?

HOW MIGHT I BECOME MORE RESPECTFUL?

THERE WAS ALSO A CONTROVERSIAL NEW PROPOSITION.

HOW MIGHT WE PUT PATIENT NEEDS FIRST IN THE SYSTEM?

WHAAA?!

AT AN OPEN CONVERSATION ON PATIENT-CENTRED CARE, I WAS SITTING WITH THE VP CLINICAL.

ONE LPN ROLLED HER EYES ANGRILY WHEN MOM REFUSED HER PILLS.

SHOULDN'T HAVE HAPPENED.

A HEALTH SERVICES MANAGER WAS ALSO THERE.

I'LL TELL YOU WHY THAT HAPPENS. MANAGING IS ALMOST IMPOSSIBLE. SOME OF US MANAGE 200 PEOPLE.

80% OF OUR WORK IS BUDGETING, SEEING HOW WE CAN CUT BACK— WHETHER WE CAN REDUCE A POSITION OR NOT. THAT'S TOP-DOWN PRESSURE.

WE ARE ALWAYS SHORT-STAFFED, RESCHEDULING IS CONSTANT. OUR BUDGETS HAVE NEVER BEEN ADEQUATE! AND BECAUSE GERIATRIC CARE DOESN'T WARRANT RNs, CARE IS NOT ALWAYS ADEQUATE EITHER.

20% OF OUR WORK IS MANAGING DIFFICULT STAFF. I DON'T EVEN KNOW WHO'S DIFFICULT! FAMILIES ARE AFRAID TO COMPLAIN AND I DON'T HAVE TIME TO MONITOR.

AND YET...

WE'LL GET RID OF BLOATED ADMINISTRATIONS AND REDIRECT THE MONEY TO MORE FRONT-LINE CARE!

VOTE FOR HIM!

VOTE FOR HIM!

YES!

POLITICIAN

EVEN THOUGH MY HUSBAND AND KIDS WERE THERE FOR ME I REALLY NEEDED MORE, ESPECIALLY MORE ANSWERS. I LOOKED TO EXPERTS.

SUSAN SEEKS AN EXPERT

IF ONLY I COULD TALK TO THEM IN PERSON...

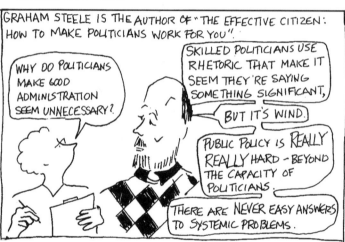

GRAHAM STEELE IS THE AUTHOR OF "THE EFFECTIVE CITIZEN: HOW TO MAKE POLITICIANS WORK FOR YOU".

WHY DO POLITICIANS MAKE GOOD ADMINISTRATION SEEM UNNECESSARY?

SKILLED POLITICIANS USE RHETORIC THAT MAKE IT SEEM THEY'RE SAYING SOMETHING SIGNIFICANT,

BUT IT'S WIND.

PUBLIC POLICY IS REALLY REALLY HARD - BEYOND THE CAPACITY OF POLITICIANS.

THERE ARE NEVER EASY ANSWERS TO SYSTEMIC PROBLEMS.

AND, OF COURSE, NO ONE IS CHEERING FOR WELL-PAID ADMINISTRATORS IN AN UNDER-FUNDED SYSTEM.

WHEN POLITICIANS SAY THEY'LL CUT ADMINISTRATIONS, PEOPLE CLAP AND CHEER.

I'VE SEEN IT!

OF COURSE, THAT DOESN'T STAND UP TO SCRUTINY.

BUT FOR POLITICIANS, IT WORKS.

HE WAS A POLITICIAN FOR 13 YEARS.

AND SO NOTHING CHANGES I GUESS.

NO WONDER PEOPLE DON'T TRUST POLITICIANS.

MY COMMUNICATIONS TEAM BEGAN HAVING ITS OWN CONVERSATIONS.

HOW MIGHT WE CHANGE OUR WORK FOR THE SAKE OF PATIENT-CENTRED CARE?

CIRCLE CONVERSATIONS WERE ENCOURAGED BECAUSE, WITHOUT A TABLE, POWER IS DIFFUSED AND HONESTY IS EASIER.

BUT IT'S SCARY.

MAYBE TOO HONEST.

SUSAN, YOU'RE VERY HARD ON YOURSELF! CHILL!

BUT I'M AN IMPOSTER. CAN'T YOU SEE THAT?

WHATEVER MY FLAWS, I WAS LOYAL TO MOM. NOW SHE NEEDED NURSING HOME CARE.

ASSISTED LIVING NON-UNION

ENHANCED SENIOR CARE

ASSISTED LIVING UNION

AFFORDABLE? HIGH QUALITY? NURSING HOME CARE

NOT READILY.

USING MY FATHER'S VETERANS' SPOUSAL BENEFIT, I GOT MOM OUT OF HOSPITAL QUICKLY AND INTO AN EXPENSIVE PRIVATE 24/7 NURSING HOME.

ONLY $8000 A MONTH

WE WERE LUCKY.

LIKE MOST FAMILIES, WE BROUGHT A LOT OF BAGGAGE.

EXPECTATIONS
MIS-UNDERSTANDING
EXHAUSTION
EMOTIONAL LABOUR
TIME
SHE LOVED YOU MORE
GRIEF
GUILT
OVERWHELM
HEALTH ISSUES
MONEY LOSS
SADNESS
TRAUMA WRONGS
OLD RESENTMENTS
PATTERNS

BUT AGAIN, NOT TALKING ABOUT WHAT'S WEIGHING US DOWN WAS TYPICAL OF MY FAMILY.

NO.

HEY YOU! CAN YOU SPARE SOME CONCERN? EMPATHY?

WHAT WAS I EXPECTING? NONETHELESS, MY BROTHER'S DETACHMENT COMPOUNDED MY FEELINGS OF LOSS AND LONELINESS. PLUS I WAS EXHAUSTED. I LOOKED TO THE INTERNET.

SUSAN SEEKS AN EXPER

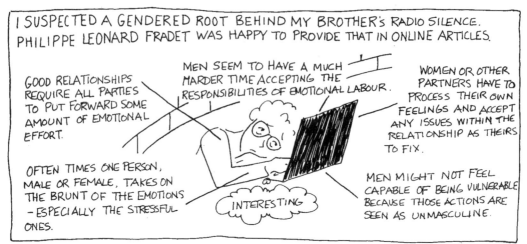

I SUSPECTED A GENDERED ROOT BEHIND MY BROTHER'S RADIO SILENCE. PHILIPPE LEONARD FRADET WAS HAPPY TO PROVIDE THAT IN ONLINE ARTICLES.

GOOD RELATIONSHIPS REQUIRE ALL PARTIES TO PUT FORWARD SOME AMOUNT OF EMOTIONAL EFFORT.

MEN SEEM TO HAVE A MUCH HARDER TIME ACCEPTING THE RESPONSIBILITIES OF EMOTIONAL LABOUR.

WOMEN OR OTHER PARTNERS HAVE TO PROCESS THEIR OWN FEELINGS AND ACCEPT ANY ISSUES WITHIN THE RELATIONSHIP AS THEIRS TO FIX.

OFTEN TIMES ONE PERSON, MALE OR FEMALE, TAKES ON THE BRUNT OF THE EMOTIONS – ESPECIALLY THE STRESSFUL ONES.

INTERESTING

MEN MIGHT NOT FEEL CAPABLE OF BEING VULNERABLE BECAUSE THOSE ACTIONS ARE SEEN AS UNMASCULINE.

WISH I'D UNDERSTOOD THAT THEN. I DID KNOW ENOUGH TO WORRY ABOUT MOM'S EMOTIONS.

MOM, I KNOW THIS MOVE IS TOUGH. I'M HERE AND WILL LOOK OUT FOR YOU.

THAT KIND OF REASSURANCE WAS FOREIGN TO MY UPBRINGING.

MOM! I HAD A NIGHTMARE! I'M SCARED!

OH GO BACK TO SLEEP! YOU HAVE NO IDEA WHAT FEAR IS!

I'M LEARNING NEW LIFE SKILLS. IT'S ALL TOO MUCH!

I'M NOT SLEEPING. I'M NOT DOING WELL BY ANYONE. I'LL RESIGN FROM MY JOB!

LITTLE DID I KNOW...

... THE PERSONAL AND SYSTEMIC WHIRLPOOLS OF WEIRDNESS WERE JUST BEGINNING.

CHAPTER SIX

NOTHING'S WRONG HERE.

THE SOCIAL WORKER WELCOMED US TO MOM'S NURSING HOME.

WELCOME TO HAPPY STONECARE!

ROOM 147

I DON'T REMEMBER HER EXACT WORDS, JUST THE ESSENCE.

THIS SHELF IS FOR ITEMS THAT HELP US KNOW MORE ABOUT YOU, DEAR.

147

LITTLE THINGS! ONLY THREE.

NOTHING OF VALUE!

YOUR THINGS MAY GET STOLEN, BUT WE MAKE SURE YOU'RE SAFE!

DEAR

SNAP

YOUR CONDITION MEANS A REVOLVING CAST OF STRANGERS WILL ATTEND TO YOUR MOST PERSONAL NEEDS.

GLAD TO HELP!

DEAR

BUT WE WILL BE DOING THAT AS OUR TIME ALLOWS.

TWO PEOPLE TO TRANSFER MRS MACLEOD

DEAR.

I HAVE TO PEE!

IT'S OK TO GO IN YOUR UNDERWEAR, DEAR. THEY'RE MADE FOR THAT!

BEFORE I LEAVE, HERE ARE A FEW PAPERS TO SIGN, DEAR.

THIS ONE GIVES US PERMISSION TO NOT RESUSCITATE YOU IF YOU HAVE A HEART ATTACK.

WHY WOULD I SIGN THAT!?

BECAUSE OLDER PEOPLE'S RIBS BREAK IF WE GIVE THEM CPR. DEAR.

WELL. THAT'S A FINE HOW D'YA DO!!

MOM DIDN'T LIKE HER ROOMMATE.

YOU! YOU'RE A VIPER!

FINALLY, AFTER TWO YEARS, WE GOT HER INTO A SINGLE ROOM IN A GOVERNMENT FUNDED PLACE.

MUST YOU GO SO SOON?

MOM WAS GLAD TO BE ON HER OWN AGAIN.

I'M VIPER-FREE.

MAJESTY

BUY THIS SET

SHE EVEN SEEMED TO LIKE THE FOOD, ALTHOUGH OTHERS DIDN'T.

THEY'RE TERRIBLE COOKS!

MEALS ARE A MAIN EVENT IN A NURSING HOME DAY. PEOPLE SIT FOR HOURS JUST WAITING FOR THE DINING ROOM TO OPEN FOR SUPPER.

DINING ROOM →

MENU

MEALS ARE ONE OF THE FEW TIMES THEY CAN EXERT SOME CONTROL...

I LIKES TO SEE IT BEFORE I EATS IT.

...AND EXPRESS AN OPINION.

DON'T EVER TAKE THE CHICKEN LEG. IT'S BONY!

ONE OF MOM'S TABLEMATES DIDN'T LIKE ME OR MY ATTEMPTS AT CHEERY CONVERSATION.

LOOK AT YOUR BIG MOUTH!

WONDER YOU DON'T CHOKE ON THAT BIG SCARF!

ANOTHER TABLEMATE DIDN'T LIKE ANYTHING AT ALL!

I HATE IT HERE!

I GUESS WE JUST HAVE TO MAKE THE BEST OF IT.

(SOLUTION SUSAN.)

I DON'T WANT TO MAKE THE BEST OF IT!!

OH.

FAIR POINT.

THE HOME WAS NEW AND BEAUTIFUL.

AND SOME STAFF WERE KIND, ESPECIALLY JANITORS.

AH, YOU'RE READING A ROYAL MAGAZINE. I SAW DIANA HERE IN '83.

OH. NO USE FOR DIANA, EH? GOT IT.

JANITORS SEEMED TO HAVE MORE DISCRETIONARY TIME. BUSY STAFF WASHED, FED AND TOILETED RESIDENTS EACH DAY. RECREATION ACTIVITIES WERE AN HOUR TWICE A DAY, WEEKDAYS ONLY. IT WAS EASIER FOR JANITORS TO BE FRIENDLY AND GENEROUS WITH THEIR TIME.

207

IS THAT MY ROOM?

IS MY FAMILY THERE?

YES.

NO.

BUT I'LL STOP BY IN A MINUTE, REG.

BEYOND THAT, MANY RESIDENTS SPENT HOURS ALONE.

SOME PEOPLE TOOK SOCIALIZING INTO THEIR OWN HANDS.

HELP.

REMEMBER THE FURNITURE STORE ON KEMPT ROAD? I WORKED THERE FOR 35 YEARS. PEOPLE WOULD COME ALL THE WAY FROM GLACE BAY AND NEW BRUNSWICK. I TREATED PEOPLE WELL. THEY COULD TRUST ME. I NEVER PUSHED THEM. MY WIFE...

PEOPLE SEEMED LONELY. I TRIED TO LEARN SOME OF THEIR NAMES.

HI. I'M SUSAN. THIS IS MY MOTHER.

I DON'T CARE.

MOSTLY, IT WAS WELCOMED.

OH MY. THIS IS YOUR MOTHER! I'M VELMA. I JUST LOVE OLD PEOPLE! HELLO DEAR.

SHE'S SO SWEET!

SOME EVEN APPRECIATED IT.

HELLO! OH WE LOVE YOU!

YOU'RE THE ONLY ONE WHO TALKS TO US.

NICE TO SEE YOU TOO, ROSE, EILEEN.

SOME TOO MUCH.

UGH.

I LOVE YA! I LOVE YA!

MOM STILL KEENLY FOLLOWED POLITICS.

PEOPLE WHO VOTE FOR HARPER ARE IDIOTS!

SHE HATED BINGO AND CONCERTS, ESPECIALLY COUNTRY MUSIC. AS SOMEONE ALERT ENOUGH TO FOLLOW AN ELECTION, SHE NEEDED TO BE ENGAGED, TO BE SEEN, TO FEEL LIKE SHE BELONGED.

I OFTEN FOUND HER ALONE, SLUMPED IN THE HALLWAY.

I WAS RELIEVED TO KNOW SHE WAS CARED FOR IN WAYS I COULDN'T POSSIBLY MANAGE.

HI MOM!

MOM?

BUT SADDENED TO SEE HER ALONE SO MUCH.

RESIDENTS SEEMED MORE PROCESSED THAN LOOKED AFTER.

MOM, YOUR NAILS ARE DIRTY AND NEED CLIPPING!

I KNOW!

THEY'RE ALWAYS TELLING ME HOW BUSY THEY ARE AND HOW MANY OTHERS THEY HAVE ON THEIR SHIFT!

I'M JUST A BOTHER TO THEM!

AND JUST WHO TEACHES CARE WORKERS TO TALK THAT WAY TO RESIDENTS?

DESPITE AGE-RELATED DECLINE AND COGNITION ISSUES, MOST RESIDENTS UNDERSTOOD HOW THEY WERE TREATED AND WHY THEY WERE THERE.

I'M NOT AFRAID OF DEATH YOU KNOW

THAT'S VERY INTERESTING. MAY I COME AND TALK TO YOU ABOUT THAT SOMETIME?

SHE WELCOMED THAT BUT BY THE TIME I GOT AROUND TO IT, SHE HAD DIED.

MARKETING FOR PRIVATE NURSING HOMES ALMOST ALWAYS FEATURES ONE-ON-ONE CARE.

ROSEHALL SENIOR CARE

CAREPLACE

♡ JUST LIKE HOME ♡

LIES, I SAY.

THE RESIDENT-CENTRED CARE I SAW WAS STAFF FRANTICALLY RUNNING IN CIRCLES AROUND SLUMPED RESIDENTS

THEY'RE LIKE CHILDREN IN ONE WAY. YOU CAN'T GIVE THEM ENOUGH ATTENTION.

HARD TO DO WHEN YOU'RE FUNDED FOR 2.45 HOURS OF HANDS-ON CARE PER RESIDENT PER DAY.

IF MARKETING WERE HONEST:

MANY LONELY HOURS. ALMOST NO ONE-ON-ONE, HANDS-ON CARE.

DAILY SCHEDULE

MORNING: OUT OF BED TOILETED, DRESSED, TO DINING ROOM. ONE ACTIVITY 10 AM

THE TIMING IS YOURS!

LUNCH: TO DINING ROOM TOILETED ONE ACTIVITY 2 PM

SUPPER: TO DINING ROOM TOILETED TO BED

BATHS ONCE-A-WEEK

CALL BELL RANDOMLY ANSWERED

MY MOTHER'S NEXT DOOR NEIGHBOUR WAS ETHEL, A WOMAN WITH THREE DAUGHTERS WHO VISITED HER REGULARLY. SHE WAS IN HER 90s.

SHE HAD HAD A SUCCESSFUL CAREER AS A MANAGER AT A LOCAL DAIRY, UNUSUAL FOR HER GENERATION.

LIKE MOM, ETHEL SUFFERED FROM VERY OLD AGE. HER DEMENTIA WAS AGE-RELATED.

MOM, CAN YOU SEE WHERE THIS CARD SHOULD GO?

NO.

ONE DAY ON MY WAY OUT, I NOTICED ETHEL WAS CRYING.

ETHEL?

I JUST DON'T KNOW WHY I'M HERE!

WHY AREN'T I HOME? IT'S JUST UP THE STREET BUT NO ONE WILL TAKE ME THERE.

HER HOME WAS FAR AWAY AND LONG GONE.

WHY HAVE MY DAUGHTERS LEFT ME HERE?

I KNOW YOUR DAUGHTERS LOVE YOU, ETHEL.

I DIDN'T KNOW WHAT ELSE TO SAY. I TOLD ETHEL I'D FIND SOMEONE TO HELP HER. (I HAD STUFF TO DO.)

EXCUSE ME. ETHEL'S CRYING IN HER ROOM.

SHE OFTEN GETS LIKE THAT. SHE'LL BE OK.

THEN SHE SHRUGGED.

I LOOKED BACK AND SAW HER GLARING AT ME ON MY WAY OUT.

SHE HAD NO INTENTION OF COMFORTING ETHEL. (SHE PROBABLY HAD STUFF TO DO.)

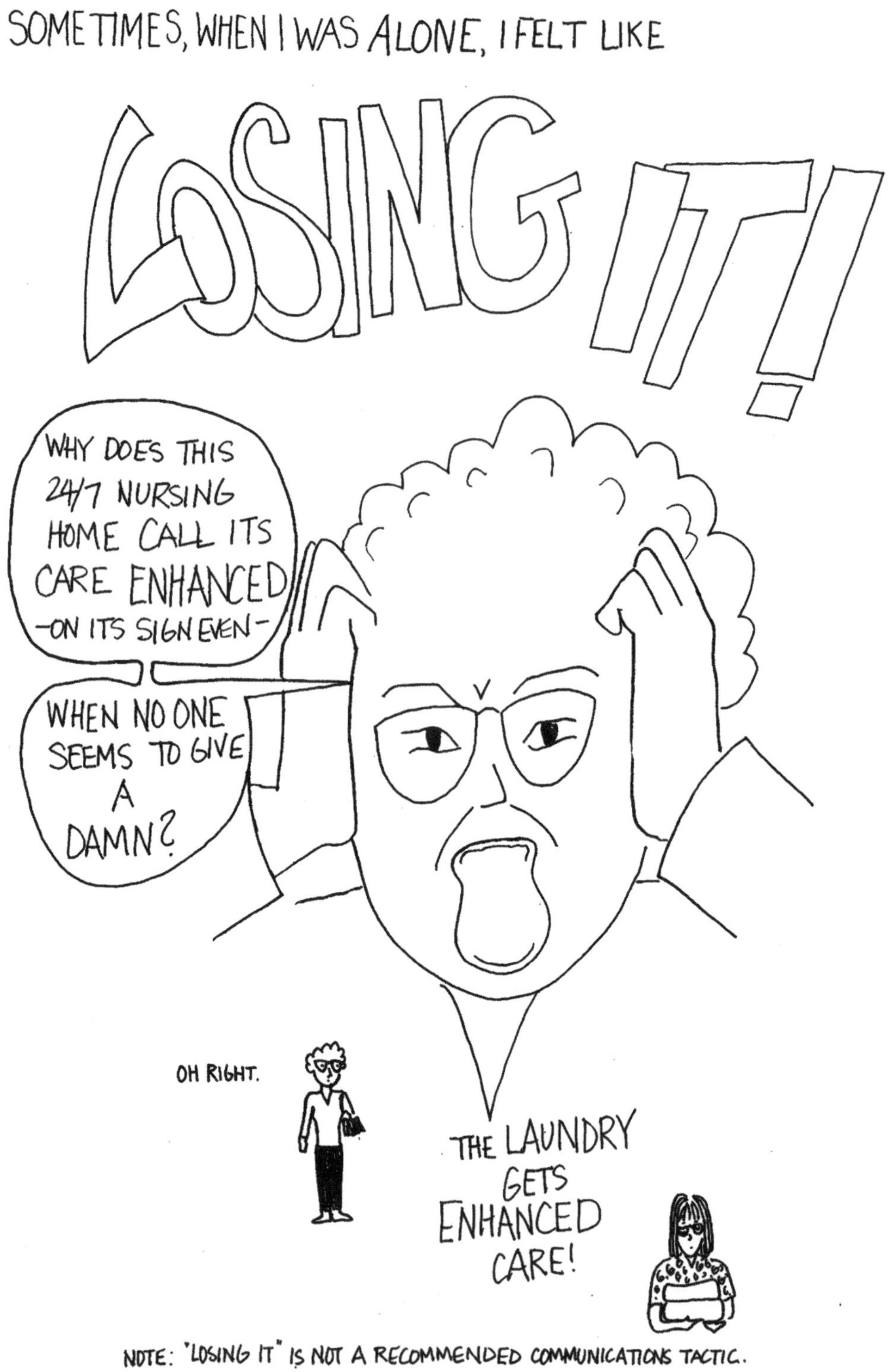
SOMETIMES, WHEN I WAS ALONE, I FELT LIKE
LOSING IT!
WHY DOES THIS 24/7 NURSING HOME CALL ITS CARE ENHANCED -ON ITS SIGN EVEN-
WHEN NO ONE SEEMS TO GIVE A DAMN?
OH RIGHT.
THE LAUNDRY GETS ENHANCED CARE!
NOTE: "LOSING IT" IS NOT A RECOMMENDED COMMUNICATIONS TACTIC.

SUSAN SEEKS AN EXPERT.

CONFUSED, I LOOKED TO MARIE-CLAIRE CHARTRAND, A LICENSED SOCIAL WORKER, CERTIFIED ELDER MEDIATOR AND PROFESSIONAL LONG-TERM CARE NAVIGATOR.

I PRETENDED TO INTERVIEW HER ON TV!

WHY WERE MY EXPECTATIONS OF NURSING HOME CARE SO OFF?

IF YOU HAVE NO EXPERIENCE IN THEM, YOU'LL HAVE NO IDEA.

THE ONLY VISUALS ARE FROM PRIVATE-PAY HOMES AND THEY'RE SELLING PEACE-OF-MIND WITH IDEALIZED IMAGES.

THE REALITY IS FAR MORE INSTITUTIONALIZED—AS YOU KNOW, SUSAN.

YOU MAY NEVER HAVE SEEN A DISABLED PERSON OTHER THAN YOUR FAMILY MEMBER. YOU'LL BE CONFRONTED WITH DIFFICULT SIGHTS AND HEAR GROANS AND YELLS, PERHAPS, FROM PEOPLE WITH DEMENTIA.

SNORT

DROOL GRRRR!

AHHHHHHHHH

TAKE ME HOME!

TAKE ME HOME!

IF SOMEONE'S HAD AN ACCIDENT, YOU'LL SMELL SOMETHING TOO. BUT BE BRAVE. SIT DOWN AND WATCH.

I REMEMBERED YOU LIKE ICE CREAM.

TELL ME ABOUT YOUR BABY.

HERE COMES THE DAY CARE!

IS THERE ALWAYS SOMETHING GOING ON? A PUB? A COMMUNITY FEELING? A SENSE OF 'INVITING IN' RATHER THAN 'KEEPING OUT'?

I'VE OBSERVED THAT VOLUNTEERS WON'T RETURN IF THEY THINK CARE IS POOR.

HERE'S A ROUGH FORMULA, FROM WHAT I'VE SEEN.

GOOD MANAGEMENT = CONTENTED STAFF AND VOLUNTEERS = GOOD CARE

WISH I'D KNOWN THAT.

AND EVERYTHING IS MADE MORE DIFFICULT BY ONGOING STAFF SHORTAGES.

OTHER RESEARCH TOLD ME THAT FOR-PROFIT LONG-TERM CARE HOMES DELIVER INFERIOR CARE ACROSS SEVERAL MEASURES. SO COMPLEX!

BUT I UNDERSTAND GOVERNMENT INACTION.

ONCE, IN MY FORMER LIFE . . .

THAT MAN CALLED ASKING FOR GOVERNMENT TO PAY FOR HIS FATHER'S SPECIAL READING LAMP IN THE NURSING HOME.

DIRECTOR

DEAR GAWD!

COMMUNICATIONS DIRECTOR

OH SURE! WHY DON'T WE PAY FOR HIS SOCKS TOO?

WE CAN BARELY AFFORD IVs! WHO DO PEOPLE THINK WE ARE?!

COMMU DIRECT

THEIR MOTHERS!!

IN GOVERNMENT, IT WAS FRUSTRATING THAT PEOPLE DIDN'T UNDERSTAND THE DIFFICULTY IN SERVING LARGE AND DIVERSE NEEDS EQUITABLY.

NOT ENOUGH REVENUE

LONG TERM CARE

HEALTH CARE

SOCIAL SERVICES

BUSINESS STIMULUS

ARTS

EDUCATION

JUSTICE

DEBT

EARLY CHILDHOOD EDUCATION

WHACK-A-MOLE.

WE THOUGHT WE WERE ALL LUCKY TO HAVE ANY SERVICES IN A HAVE-NOT JURISDICTION.

CLEAN WATER

SCHOOLS

HOSPITAL

ROADS

VERY POOR COUNTRY

YOU SHOULD BE GRATEFUL!

I WAS THE COMMUNICATIONS POINT PERSON WHEN A LOCAL DIOCESE NEEDED TO CLOSE THEIR MOTHERHOUSE HOUSING ELDERLY NUNS – IN WINTER.

THE BEAUTIFUL BUILDING WAS TOO OLD AND EXPENSIVE FOR GOVERNMENT TO CONVERT INTO A MODERN NURSING HOME. AND...

WE DON'T NEED ANY MORE SPACE!

THE NUNS WERE MOVED TO A NEWLY OPENED HOME.

WITH THEIR VERY OWN CHAPEL!

HERE'S HOW THOSE MESSAGES PLAYED IN THE MEDIA.

THEY'LL BE FINE.

TRASH

THERE WAS A PUBLIC OUTCRY AND BAD PRESS.

HOW DOES SUSAN MACLEOD SLEEP AT NIGHT?

LETTERS TO THE EDITOR

VERY WELL. I WAS EXHAUSTED.

GENERALLY, THE NUNS FARED WELL IN THEIR NEW HOME. MANY OF THEIR VOLUNTEERS FOLLOWED THEM THERE.

AND WE KNOW THE IMPORTANCE OF VOLUNTEERS TO THE SYSTEM!

THAT NURSING HOME WAS WHERE MOM ENDED UP.

LOOK, THEY'LL BE FINE!

AS A GOVERNMENT EMPLOYEE, MY BIGGEST TAKE-AWAY WAS THAT PEOPLE COMPLAINED ABOUT COMPLEX ISSUES THEY DIDN'T UNDERSTAND.

PEOPLE DON'T KNOW WHAT'S GOOD FOR THEM.

NO INDEED

WE'RE UP HERE TO HELP.

AT THE TIME I KEPT A DIARY TO RELIEVE STRESS.

DEAR DIARY,
IN MY OFFICE, WE OFTEN RECEIVE WRATHFUL LETTERS FROM THE OUTRAGED INDIGNANT WITH LITTLE GRASP OF THE FACTS.

CRITICISM, I FEEL SHOULD BE MARGINALLY INFORMED.

WHEN I RETIRE I SHALL REMEMBER THIS AND WRITE LETTERS THANKING POLITICIANS FOR TAKING ON INTRACTABLE ISSUES.

I SHALL THANK THE SYSTEM!

TODAY, RETIRED, I'VE CHANGED MY TUNE.

HA HA HA HA HA HAHAHA HAHA HA

NUMBERS WORK WELL IN COMMUNICATIONS. THEIR AUTHORITY SHUTS PEOPLE UP.

$32.8 MILLION INCREASE   96.7% SATISFACTION   32% REDUCTION IN WAIT TIMES

PEOPLE'S EXPERIENCE TELL THEM SOMETHING DIFFERENT. BUT WHO CAN RESEARCH REBUTTALS TO SYSTEM-THINKING?

YOU CAN'T FEEL BY NUMBERS. YOU CAN'T SPEAK CLEARLY WHEN YOU'RE EMOTIONAL. HUMANS = VULNERABLE SYSTEMS = IMPENETRABLE.

HUMAN SYSTEM

AS A HUMAN, IT WAS EXASPERATING AND HURTFUL TO SEE MY MOTHER SIMPLY PROCESSED BY A SYSTEM.

ERROR   BUDGET

BUT MORE DOWN-TO-EARTH, I FOUND IT INFURIATING THAT MY MOTHER'S CALL BELL WAS FREQUENTLY PLACED BEYOND HER REACH! WTF!

CALL BELL!

MOM

I HAVE TO PEEEE!

I REMEMBER TALKING TO MOM.

I DON'T LIKE THE ATTITUDE AROUND HERE.

ABOUT WHAT?

EVERYTHING

FOR ABOUT A YEAR, I MADE POLITE INQUIRIES ABOUT KEEPING HER CALL BELL NEAR HER.

EXCUSE ME, MOM HAS TO PEE.

WHO'S MOM?

STAFF ARE ON BREAK.

MONTH AFTER MONTH, I RECEIVED POLITE BUT NON-COMMITTAL RESPONSES.

AND HER CALL BELL'S STILL NOT IN SIGHT.

OH SORRY. DON'T KNOW HOW IT GOT STUCK BACK HERE.

SOLUTION SUSAN STRIKES

AS A FORMER COMMUNICATIONS PROFESSIONAL, I HAD A QUIVER OF ARROWS AT MY DISPOSAL.

THIS CALLS FOR AN ANGRY LETTER. IT'S BEEN A YEAR!

STILL NO CALL BELL WITHIN REACH

TO: NURSING HOME SOCIAL WORKER
FROM: SUSAN MACLEOD
RE: MOM'S CALL BELL

I FEEL AS A FAMILY MEMBER I AM LOOKED UPON WITH POLITE CONTEMPT AND IGNORED IF POSSIBLE.

LATER, I RAN INTO THE SOCIAL WORKER.

I'M SORRY FOR THE TONE IN MY E-MAIL.

OH, THAT'S OK. WE KNOW YOU HAVE TO DO THAT.

PAT PAT

AT HOME, I LOST IT!

THAT'S YOUR POLICY!? WAIT UNTIL WE BREAK?

I ALSO BEGAN WRITING TO MY BROTHER.

CHAPTER SEVEN

PEOPLE, EH?

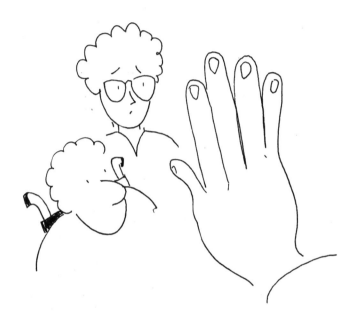

WHAT'S BURIED BENEATH
THE STORIES WE TELL
OURSELVES AND EACH OTHER?

WHAT WE WANT TO HEAR,
WHAT WE DON'T WANT TO SEE.

AFTER MOM WAS SETTLED IN, MY BROTHER CAME TO VISIT. HE WAS IN TOWN FOR A CONFERENCE

THERE ARE NO FILTERS IN OLD AGE.

SO! WHERE WERE YOU THROUGH ALL THIS!?

HE WAS ANNOYED SHE ASKED.

I LIVE ON THE OTHER SIDE OF THE COUNTRY!

FAIR POINT.

I SECRETLY CHEERED MOM.

ME TEAM

HE HAD HIS REASONS FOR BEING UNRESPONSIVE.

JOB STRESS

HEALTH STRESS

LACK OF MONEY

PARENTING STRESS

DISTANCE STRESS

SOS

OK. THAT'S WHAT IT'S LIKE TO BE YOU RIGHT NOW. GOT IT.

JOB STR

HEALTH STRESS

HIS KIDS WERE YOUNG THEN AND THAT'S BUSY. HIS JOB HELPING PEOPLE COULD CERTAINLY BE STRESSFUL.

'TIL NEXT TIME.

AND I WASN'T COMPLETELY AGAINST THE WALL THEN. BURN-OUT WOULD TAKE ANOTHER YEAR.

FINALLY, MOM'S CALL BELL WAS PLACED WITHIN HER REACH MORE OFTEN.

BUT ANSWERED?

BUZZ
BUZZ
BUZZ
BUZZ

ANYBODY OUT THERE?

I HAVE TO PEE!

BACK TO MOM'S SOCIAL WORKER.

CALL ME FUSSY - MOM'S CALL BELL IS NEAR MOM NOW. THANK YOU! BUT SHOULDN'T IT BE ANSWERED?

SHE SUGGESTED I WRITE TO THE FUNDER.

WE CAN'T HIRE ENOUGH STAFF NOW THAT THE FUNDER INSISTS WE ONLY ADMIT THE VERY FRAILEST. AND THEY EACH NEED MORE TIME FOR THE MOST BASIC CARE.

AND...

WITHIN A BUDGET THAT KEEP GETTING CUT!

THE FUNDER WAS MY OLD EMPLOYER - THE DEPARTMENT OF HEALTH.

I WAS USED TO WRITING FORMAL LETTERS FOR THE DEPARTMENT OF HEALTH.

THIS I CAN GET MY TEETH INTO!

I AM WRITING WITH RESPECT. MY MOTHER IS AMONG THE VULNERABLE, VERY OLD AND FRAIL.
PLEASE TAKE THE TIME TO CONSIDER MY COMMENTS.

HER CALL BELL IS OFTEN NOT WITHIN HER REACH AND WHEN IT IS, IT IS NOT ANSWERED IN A TIMELY FASHION. SHE RINGS THE BELL FOR THE WASHROOM OR BECAUSE SHE IS LONELY.

I ENJOYED WRITING TO THE DEPARTMENT OF HEALTH.

FREQUENTLY, I STAND IN AN EMPTY CORRIDOR WITH MY MOTHER WHO NEEDS TO PEE URGENTLY. NO ONE'S AROUND AND I'M NOT ALLOWED TO HELP HER.

WORKERS CONTINUOUSLY TELL MY MOTHER SHE'S NOT THE ONLY ONE THEY CARE FOR TO DISCOURAGE HER FROM RINGING THE CALL BELL.

I'M PEEING!

PLEASE TELL ME THE INDUSTRY STANDARD TIME TO ANSWER A CALL BELL.

YOURS SINCERELY,

SUBTEXT: YOU NEED TO FUND FOR MORE COMPASSIONATE AND BETTER TRAINED STAFF.

THE DEPARTMENT BUREAUCRAT WHO WROTE BACK MAY NOT HAVE LOOKED LIKE ME ...

... BUT WE SOUNDED A LOT ALIKE. WORDY. COLD.

THE DEPARTMENT PROVIDES A BUDGET TO THE FACILITY, IDENTIFYING THE FUNDING PROVIDED FOR EACH STAFFING GROUP.

SUBTEXT: IT'S THE MONEY STUPID.

THERE ARE VARIATIONS IN THE NUMBER OF POSITIONS PER HOME BASED ON SEVERAL FACTORS SUCH AS THE PHYSICAL SIZE OF THE FACILITY AND THE NUMBER OF RESIDENT BEDS.

SUBTEXT: WE USE NUMBERS TO DEFINE CARE.

ME: ... AS IF...

BUZZ
BUZZ
BUZZ

REGARDING A STANDARD TIME FOR WHICH A CALL BELL SHOULD BE ANSWERED: THIS IS NOT A STANDARD SET BY GOVERNMENT. PLEASE REFER TO THE FACILITY FOR THEIR POLICY.

SUBTEXT: WE'RE NOT TOUCHING THAT WITH A TEN-FOOT POLE.

I WOULD ENCOURAGE YOU TO BRING YOUR CONCERNS TO THE FACILITY ADMINISTRATION FOR FURTHER DISCUSSION.

THEY TOLD ME TO WRITE YOU!

SO THIS IS HOW "COMMUNICATIONS" WORKS.

IT'S NOT OUR FAULT!

THE BUREAUCRAT ENDED ON A CHEERFUL NOTE JUST LIKE I USED TO WHEN I WROTE GOVERNMENT CORRESPONDENCE. NEW ME AND OLD ME DID NOT LIKE EACH OTHER MUCH.

THANK YOU FOR TAKING THE TIME TO WRITE.

I WISH YOU AND YOUR MOTHER THE BEST.

I DON'T BELIEVE YOU.

SOLUTION SUSAN STRIKES

HMMM

WHAT NEXT?

AH-HA!

FACE-TO-FACE MEETING!

I ASKED FOR A MEETING WITH THE NURSING HOME EXECUTIVE DIRECTOR AND SOCIAL WORKER.

HEY, ANY STAFF WHO WORK WITH MOM CAN COME TOO!

I HAD A "THREE-PRONG" AGENDA BECAUSE THAT'S THE WAY PEOPLE TALK IN ADMINISTRATIONS.

THESE ARE MY PRONGS.

1. COMMUNICATIONS AND NAVIGATION. IS THERE ONE PERSON I CAN GO TO FOR ALL OF MOM'S NEEDS? NO ONE PERSON KNOWS HER.
2. WHY DOES HER CALL BELL GO UNANSWERED SO OFTEN?
3. RECREATION? NO ONE SEEMS TO SEE HER AS AN INDIVIDUAL. NO ONE PERSON KNOWS HER.

I ALSO BROUGHT ALONG A FRIEND WHO WAS A NURSE IN CASE I COULDN'T UNDERSTAND THE MEDICAL LANGUAGE.

SHE UNDERSTANDS YOUR LANGUAGE

AND I BROUGHT EXPENSIVE ENGLISH SHORTBREAD COOKIES.

AFTER NERVOUS SMALL TALK, I REVIEWED MY CONCERNS. YOU CAN GUESS THE RESPONSE.

WELL, THE CHALLENGE IS...

... HOW DO YOU CHANGE THE PATIENT EXPERIENCE WHEN YOU ARE ONLY FUNDED FOR 2.45 HOURS OF CARE PER 24 HOURS PER RESIDENT?

THAT BARELY COVERS MOBILIZING THEM IN THE MORNING, TOILETING THEM, FEEDING THEM, DISPENSING MEDS AND RESPONDING TO URGENT NEEDS.

WE WORK THE ABSOLUTE HARDEST TO DO WHAT WE CAN!

SUBTEXT: IT'S THE FAULT OF GOVERNMENT FUNDING. MONEY.

AND WHEN YOU WRITE TO THE DEPARTMENT OF HEALTH, IT ONLY CREATES HEAPS OF PAPERWORK FOR US.

YEAH

IS SHE TELLING ME TO STOP WRITING TO THE GOVERNMENT

EVEN THOUGH THE SOCIAL WORKER TOLD ME TOO?

YUP. YOU'VE BEEN TOLD.

THERE WAS NOT MUCH MORE TO SAY. IT TURNED OUT MY FRIEND AND THE EXECUTIVE DIRECTOR WENT TO NURSING SCHOOL TOGETHER.

BOY. DO WE GO BACK A LONG WAY!

TIME FLIES!

THE EXECUTIVE DIRECTOR SEEMED TO RELAX AND FEEL SAFE WITH A FRIENDLY NURSE IN THE ROOM.

I USED TO LOOK DOWN ON LONG-TERM CARE NURSING.

MAYBE THE SHORTBREAD SOFTENED HER TOO.

WAS I WRONG! EACH PERSON LIVING HERE HAS A MULTITUDE OF SERIOUS HEALTH ISSUES.

SHE BECAME MORE HUMAN.

SHE OPENED UP. BUT I DID NOT EXPECT SHE WOULD SAY...

YOU KNOW, EVERYONE WORKING HERE IS JUST TRYING TO PROTECT THEIR HEALTH CARE ASSES! WE'RE CHECKING OFF ALL THE GOVERNMENT BOXES THAT TELL US WHAT WE'RE SUPPOSED TO DO IN THE COURSE OF A SHIFT — WITHOUT ENOUGH RESOURCES!

I WAS STUNNED!

THEY DON'T TALK THAT WAY IN THE MARKETING BROCHURES.

TO ME, THAT EXPRESSED A FEAR OF THE FUNDER RATHER THAN A COMMITMENT TO RESIDENT WELLBEING.

SO... THIS IS HOW THE SYSTEM REALLY WORKS.

TICKING BOXES!

IT ALSO BEGGED THE QUESTION:

WHAT ABOUT MY MOTHER'S ASS?

I'M PEEING!

THE MORE I LEARNED ABOUT THE COLD SYSTEM, THE WARMER I BECAME TO MOM.

I BEGAN TO COMMUNICATE WITH HER IN THE WAYS SHE WANTED, NOT THE WAYS I DID. MOM'S PASSION WAS HISTORY, A SUBJECT THAT ALWAYS BORED ME STIFF.

WHAT INTERESTS YOU MOST ABOUT ALEXANDER GRAHAM BELL, MOM?

WELL, HE WAS BRILLIANT AND HE LOVED HIS WIFE MABEL DEARLY.

RELUCT GENIUS CHARLOTTE GRE

SHE READ A LOT, USED TO LOVE CROSSWORDS AND WAS NEVER FAR AWAY FROM A DICTIONARY. I BROUGHT IN SCRABBLE TILES - SHE STILL HAD IT!

MY DAUGHTER SENT HER FUNNY POSTCARDS FROM ENGLAND.

I LOVE THAT! HEE HEE

GOD SAVE THE QUEEN

I FOUND OLD FAMILY THINGS.

LOOK MOM!

OH! I HAVEN'T SEEN THAT IN AGES!

SLOWLY OUR RELATIONSHIP BECAME MORE THAN ME AND MY TASTES, COMFORT LEVELS AND EXPECTATIONS OF HER.

LET'S GO LISTEN TO THE CELTIC MUSIC.

THAT'S YOUR IDEA OF FUN?

MUSIC TODAY

AND I BEGAN TO TAKE HER EXPECTATIONS OF ME IN STRIDE. SHE DIDN'T THREATEN ME ANYMORE.

I'LL BE GLAD WHEN THIS BIG SCARF TREND IS OVER.

WILL YOU, MOM?

IT WAS EXHAUSTING TO PAY SUCH ATTENTION.

MOM WANTS A NEW SWEATER, HIP-LENGTH, FLORAL PATTERN, SNAPS NOT BUTTONS IN TEAL BLUE WITH A V-NECK.

eBay

SIGH.

WHILE A NEW AFFECTION WAS GROWING BETWEEN MOM AND ME, SOMETHING ELSE WAS GROWING BETWEEN MY BROTHER AND ME.

NO COMMENT.

MOM REALLY LIKED THE NEW SWEATER I GOT HER. MAYBE YOU COULD SEND HER SOMETHING — MAYBE GREETING CARDS REGULARLY LIKE G. DOES.

MOM'S HEALTH BEGAN TO WORSEN — MORE INFECTIONS AND MORE HOSPITAL VISITS.

HI SUSAN. NICE TO SEE YOU AGAIN.

I WAS ALWAYS CALLED TO GO ALONG.

I WAS SURPRISED HOW MUCH TIME AND ENERGY THIS ALL TOOK.

SUSAN SEEKS AN EXPERT

BECAUSE I WAS SPENDING A LOT OF TIME IN BED, I BEGAN TO DO MY RESEARCH THERE. I FOUND A PERTINENT BOOK BY DR. THOMAS R COLE.

THOMAS R COLE
OLD MAN COUNTRY
MY SEARCH FOR MEANING AMONG THE ELDERS.

HE WROTE: IF YOU ARE AN AGING CHILD OF AN AGING PARENT, YOUR JOB DESCRIPTION IS:

- DECIDE WHEN AND HOW MUCH TO INTERVENE AS YOUR PARENT BECOMES COMPROMISED.

- WORK WITH PHYSICIANS AND CAREGIVERS TO DEVISE SAFE AND RESPECTFUL SYSTEMS OF CARE.

- BECOME AWARE THAT YOU WILL REVERT TO PAINFUL PATTERNS OF EMOTIONS FROM YOUR CHILDHOOD. (!)

SIGH. NO WONDER I'M WEARY.

- MANAGE THE FEAR, ANXIETY AND RESENTMENT PROVOKED BY YOUR PARENT'S FLUCTUATING COMPETENCY.

- WORK WITH YOUR SIBLINGS TO CREATE, WHEN POSSIBLE, CONSENSUS ABOUT MAJOR DECISIONS. (!)

REMEMBER YOUR PARENT'S WELLBEING IS PRIMARY.

I KEPT MY BROTHER INFORMED WITH LITTLE RESPONSE. INCREASINGLY THIS SADDENED ME.

HIS TYPICAL REPLY.

THANKS FOR KEEPING ME INFORMED.

I NEEDED VALIDATION FROM SOMEWHERE. MOM'S OTHER CHILD SEEMED THE LIKELY SOURCE.

HOW DO I GET THROUGH TO HIM? I WANT LOVE AND ATTENTION FROM HIM, DAMN IT! MOM DOES TOO!

I WANTED HIM TO UNDERSTAND I FELT I WAS DOING THIS ON HIS BEHALF TOO. I WAS FEELING INVISIBLE. AND WEIGHED DOWN.

HELP.

I FELT GUILTY ABOUT HOW MUCH I HAD BULLIED HIM. THERE WASN'T MUCH TO LEARN FROM MY FAMILY'S COMMUNICATIONS.

MY ATTEMPTS AT REACHING OUT TO MY BROTHER WERE WEAK AT BEST.

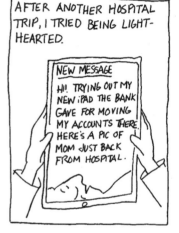

AFTER ANOTHER HOSPITAL TRIP, I TRIED BEING LIGHT-HEARTED.

NEW MESSAGE

HI! TRYING OUT MY NEW iPAD THE BANK GAVE FOR MOVING MY ACCOUNTS THERE. HERE'S A PIC OF MOM JUST BACK FROM HOSPITAL.

FOR ONCE, HE WROTE BACK SWIFTLY, NOT MENTIONING MOM.

BANKS! CREDIT UNIONS ARE MUCH BETTER IF YOU HAVE ANY SENSE OF COMMUNITY!

G

WELL, I ASKED FOR THAT.

I TRIED HUMOUR BEFORE VALENTINE'S DAY.

O

HAVE YOU CONSIDERED SENDING MOM FLOWERS? WE HAVE A FRIEND WHO OWNS A NEW FLOWER SHOP. IF YOU'RE THINKING OF SENDING MOM FLOWERS ON VALENTINE'S DAY, GO TO THIS SHOP.

IF YOU WERE THINKING OF SENDING FLOWERS TO MOM ON VALENTINE'S DAY, I'M SURE IT WOULD CHEER HER UP AND HELP HER RECALL YOUR LOVE.

IF YOU WERE THINKING OF SENDING MOM FLOWERS ON VALENTINE'S DAY, SHE LIKES ROSES.

HE WROTE BACK CALLING MY MESSAGE "GUILT-INDUCING HUMOUR", BUT THAT IT GOT HIM THINKING.

I'M SURPRISED NOW I DIDN'T RECOGNIZE IT AS "GUILT-INDUCING".

MOM NEVER RECEIVED FLOWERS FROM HIM.

MY INTENTION WAS NOT TO MAKE HIM FEEL GUILTY. I LONGED FOR A GENUINE RESPONSE TO THE STRUGGLES MOM AND I WERE HAVING.

I DEMAND ATTENTION! SO DOES MOM!

DAMN IT!

THE NEXT TIME MY BROTHER WAS IN TOWN...

SO MANY YEARS APART! WE DON'T KNOW EACH OTHER VERY WELL.

WHY DON'T WE FACETIME ONCE A MONTH?

YEAH. OK.

I WAS PROUD I HAD COME UP WITH A WAY TO BRING US CLOSER.

SOLUTION SUSAN STRIKES!

THE LOOK ON HIS FACE PUZZLED ME THOUGH.

WE FACETIMED MAYBE FOUR TIMES. WE BOTH SEEMED UNCOMFORTABLE AND THE CALLS TRAILED OFF.

MOM'S DEMANDS GREW.

SHE'S STARTED SCRATCHING PEOPLE DURING HER SHOWER.

OH! I'M SO SORRY!

IT'S OK. SHE'S JUST REACHING ANOTHER STAGE.

MY ANNOYANCE AT MY BROTHER'S NON-INVOLVEMENT GREW TOO. COINCIDENCE?

AND WHEN HE DOES COME, HE SPENDS MORE TIME VISITING OUR HOME TOWN THAN WITH MOM!

I CAN SEE HOW MUCH THIS UPSETS YOU.

YEARS WERE PASSING BUT HE STILL RESPONDED TO ME IN THE SAME WAYS. I BEGAN TO SEE HIS TALK AS DEFLECTION.

HEALTH STRESS

JOB STRESS

LACK OF MONEY

DISTANCE STRESS

PARENTING STRESS

IT'S NOT MY RESPONSIBILITY!

I COULD ALSO HEAR A WHISPERING VOICE OF REASON.

IT'S NORMAL HE WOULDN'T WANT TO BE CONTROLLED BY A BULLYING OLDER SISTER. AND YOU'RE NOT THE MOST GENEROUS INTERPRETER OF HIS MOTIVES.

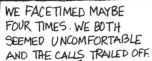

IT'S EASY TO LOOK AT THE SURFACE OF SOMEONE ELSE YET EXPECT THEM TO LOOK DEEPER AT US.

HUH?

SHHH

BUT RATHER THAN LISTEN TO THAT VOICE, I TURNED TO AN EXPERT.

ANNE TUMLINSON IS AN EXPERT IN HOW THE UNITED STATES PAYS AND CARES FOR ITS OLDEST ADULTS.

SUSAN SEEKS AN EXPERT

I INVITE HER INTO MY IMAGINARY TV STUDIO.

IS IT JUST ME? AM I EXPECTING TOO MUCH?

WOMEN TEND TO THINK THAT, BUT ELDERCARE IS AN EMOTIONAL CHALLENGE.

CARING FOR AN AGING PARENT IS A SIGNIFICANT LIFE PASSAGE, MORE THAN WE RECOGNIZE AND MUCH DIFFERENT AND HARDER THAN RAISING A CHILD.

BUT MOM IS LIVING IN A HOME. I HAVE SUPPORT. SHOULDN'T THAT BE EASIER?

CARING FOR A FRAIL ELDERLY PARENT REQUIRES A HIGH AMOUNT OF EMOTIONAL ENGAGEMENT THAT ONLY A FAMILY MEMBER CAN PROVIDE.

EVEN IF YOU HAVE THE MONEY TO PAY FOR A CAREGIVER, IT DOESN'T MEAN YOUR PARENTS WANT THEM.

REMEMBER, THERE'S NO ONE-ON-ONE CARE IN A NURSING HOME.

SPEAKING OF WHICH, FOR A YEAR I HAD HIRED A CAREGIVER TO VISIT MOM TWICE A WEEK SO THAT SHE'D HAVE ME AND THE VISITOR ALMOST EVERY DAY. AFTER SOME RESISTANCE, MY BROTHER AGREED TO PAY FOR HALF OF THE VISITS.

WHY DON'T YOU JUST TAKE THE MONEY OUT OF YOUR MOTHER'S BANK ACCOUNT?

A FRIEND →

BECAUSE I WANT TO MAKE HIM PAY!

I WAS DESCENDING SLOWLY BUT SURELY FROM WOUNDED CHILD TO WOUNDED ADULT.

CHAPTER EIGHT

SO HARD

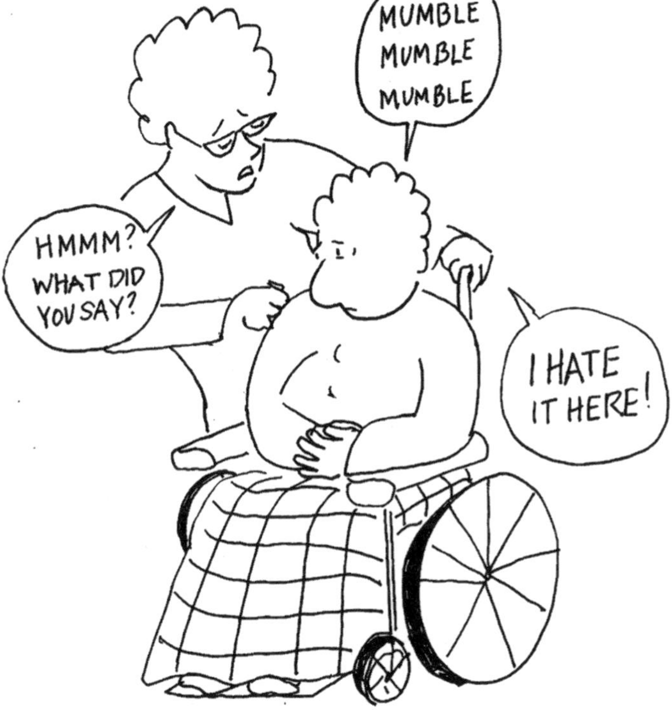
MUMBLE
MUMBLE
MUMBLE
HMMM? WHAT DID YOU SAY?
I HATE IT HERE!

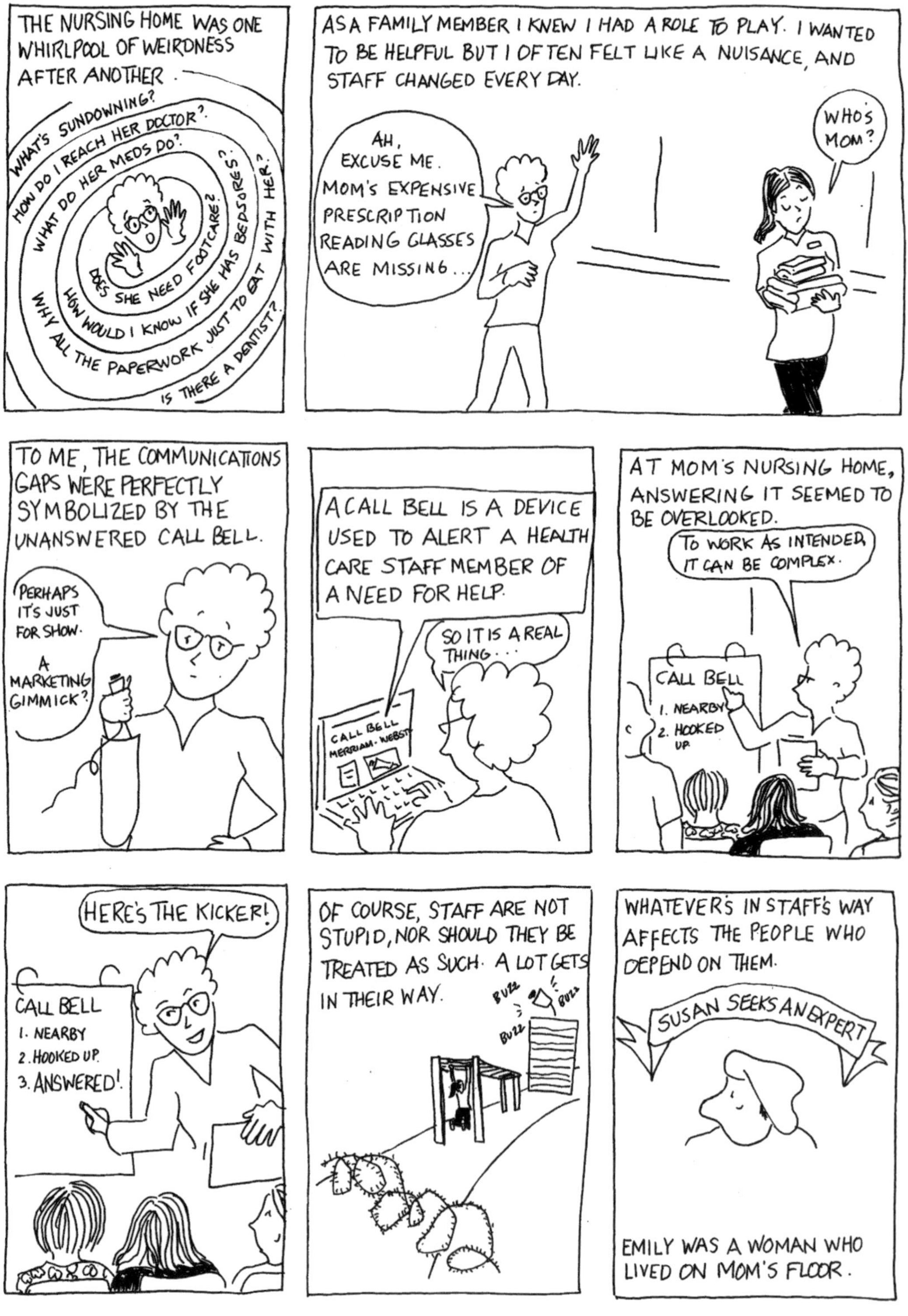
THE NURSING HOME WAS ONE WHIRLPOOL OF WEIRDNESS AFTER ANOTHER.
WHAT'S SUNDOWNING?
HOW DO I REACH HER DOCTOR?
WHAT DO HER MEDS DO?
DOES SHE NEED FOOTCARE?
HOW WOULD I KNOW IF SHE HAS BEDSORES?
WHY ALL THE PAPERWORK JUST TO EAT WITH HER?
IS THERE A DENTIST?
AS A FAMILY MEMBER I KNEW I HAD A ROLE TO PLAY. I WANTED TO BE HELPFUL BUT I OFTEN FELT LIKE A NUISANCE, AND STAFF CHANGED EVERY DAY.
AH, EXCUSE ME. MOM'S EXPENSIVE PRESCRIPTION READING GLASSES ARE MISSING...
WHO'S MOM?
TO ME, THE COMMUNICATIONS GAPS WERE PERFECTLY SYMBOLIZED BY THE UNANSWERED CALL BELL.
PERHAPS IT'S JUST FOR SHOW. A MARKETING GIMMICK?
A CALL BELL IS A DEVICE USED TO ALERT A HEALTH CARE STAFF MEMBER OF A NEED FOR HELP.
CALL BELL
MERRIAM-WEBST
SO IT IS A REAL THING...
AT MOM'S NURSING HOME, ANSWERING IT SEEMED TO BE OVERLOOKED.
TO WORK AS INTENDED, IT CAN BE COMPLEX.
CALL BELL
1. NEARBY
2. HOOKED UP
HERE'S THE KICKER!
CALL BELL
1. NEARBY
2. HOOKED UP
3. ANSWERED!
OF COURSE, STAFF ARE NOT STUPID, NOR SHOULD THEY BE TREATED AS SUCH. A LOT GETS IN THEIR WAY.
BUZZ
BUZZ
BUZZ
WHATEVER'S IN STAFF'S WAY AFFECTS THE PEOPLE WHO DEPEND ON THEM.
SUSAN SEEKS AN EXPERT
EMILY WAS A WOMAN WHO LIVED ON MOM'S FLOOR.

EMILY, WHAT'S YOUR EXPERIENCE WITH THE CALL BELL?

OH! THE CALL BELL!

I RING IT AND RING IT! 20 MINUTES! AND YOU'RE STUCK ON THE TOILET SEAT!

YOU CAN'T MOVE. YOUR LEGS HURT. YOUR BACK HURTS!

YOU HAVE TO TURN YOURSELF AROUND TO SEE IF THE BUZZER'S LIGHT IS FLASHING 'CAUSE YOU CAN'T SEE IT.

AT LEAST I'M ON THIS SIDE OF THE GRASS...

WHATEVER THAT MEANS.

SO, AS WELL AS HAVING THE CALL BELL NEARBY AND HOOKED UP, IT ALSO REQUIRED...

SOMEONE TO CARE THAT THIS SYSTEM WASN'T WORKING COMPASSIONATELY. OR BARELY AT ALL!

ANOTHER PRIVATE MOMENT OF LOSING IT!

IT TURNED OUT MOM WAS WHAT THEY CALL A "HEAVY RINGER."

DO YOU NEED TO USE THE BATHROOM?

NO!

I IMAGINE MOM KNEW SHE WANTED SOMETHING, PROBABLY NOTHING A CARE WORKER COULD PROVIDE.

MAYBE SHE WANTED HER LOST AUTONOMY, HER ABILITY TO GET UP AND GO, SOME ENERGY, TO DO AS SHE PLEASED. OR PERHAPS SHE WANTED TO HAVE A PURPOSE, TO BE VALUED, TO ENJOY SOME ATTENTION.

LONGING IS A NORMAL HUMAN IMPULSE, ESPECIALLY IF YOU CAN'T GET OUT OF YOUR CHAIR BY YOURSELF... OR ARE OFTEN ALONE.

ON THE SYSTEM SIDE, NURSING HOME STAFF CAN FIND THEMSELVES ON THE RECEIVING END OF A STAGGERING NUMBER OF ALERTS.

MANY OF THEM ARE TERMED CLINICALLY INCONSEQUENTIAL AND STAFF BECOME DESENSITIZED TO THEM.

OFF TO BREAK!

IT'S CALLED ALARM FATIGUE. RESEARCH SHOWS AN UNANSWERED CALL BELL CAUSES ANXIETY IN BOTH STAFF AND RESIDENTS.

I HAVE TO PEEEE!!

WORSE: ALARM FATIGUE HAS BEEN LINKED TO DEATH AND INJURY!

SOME SUGGEST BIOMEDICAL ENGINEERS DEVELOP ALARM ALGORITHMS THAT DETECT TRUE NEED.

I GUESS THAT'S CHEAPER THAN HIRING MORE STAFF SO THERE'S MORE TIME FOR COMPASSIONATE HUMAN-TO-HUMAN CARE, EH?

GRRRR

I DON'T KNOW WHY ENGINEERS CHOOSE THEIR PROFESSION, BUT MANY PEOPLE CHOOSE HEALTH CARE BECAUSE THEY WANT TO HELP PEOPLE DIRECTLY.

BUT ALL TOO SOON BURNOUT STRIKES MANY. I WONDERED WHY PEOPLE WHO WANT TO BE COMPASSIONATE LOSE THAT DESIRE.

SUSAN SEEKS AN EXPERT

DR. ROBIN YOUNGSON.

HE'S A NEW ZEALAND ANAESTHETIC SPECIALIST RENOWNED INTERNATIONALLY FOR PROMOTING COMPASSION IN HUMAN-CENTERED HEALTH CARE.

HIS BOOK

TIME TO CARE

HOW TO LOVE YOUR PATIENTS AND YOUR JOB.

I PRETEND TO INTERVIEW HIM.

DR. YOUNGSON, WHY DO MANY HEALTH CARE WORKERS LOSE THEIR COMPASSION OVER TIME?

THEY'RE DEEPLY IMMERSED IN A WORKPLACE CULTURE THAT INHIBITS COMPASSION.

THERE'S THE PACE, MANY COMPETING DEMANDS AND THE PERCEIVED NEED FOR OBJECTIVITY.

WHEREAS THE LATEST ADVANCES IN NEURO-SCIENCE PAINT A RICH PICTURE OF THE DEEP INTER-CONNECTION BETWEEN HUMANS...

... MEDICAL TECHNOLOGY HAS DE-HUMANIZED CARE, AS HAVE THE RULES AND POLICIES OFTEN BASED ON EFFICIENCY AND BUDGETS.

SO AN UNANSWERED CALL BELL IS A SYMPTOM OF A LARGER SOCIETAL ATTITUDE TOWARD CARE?

YOUR WORDS, BUT COULD BE.

AND SO

SUSAN SEEKS AN EXPERT AGAIN

CAREGIVERS ARE AN UNDERSTUDIED GROUP. I WANTED TO KNOW MORE ABOUT HOW THEY VIEW THEIR JOBS. I SPOKE TO A CONTINUING CARE ASSISTANT AT A LOCAL NURSING HOME.

TELL ME PLEASE, WHY DID YOU CHOOSE THIS WORK, AND WHAT ARE YOUR THOUGHTS ON ITS VALUE?

I TOOK STOCK OF MY PERSONALITY WHEN I FIRST CAME TO CANADA SIX YEARS AGO.

I REALIZED I AM A GENUINELY CARING PERSON. I ALSO KNEW MY GRANDMOTHERS DIDN'T GET THE CARE I WOULD HAVE WANTED THEM TO, SO I WANTED TO WORK WITH SENIORS.

ONE-ON-ONE CARE IS IMPORTANT TO US WORKERS AND TO RESIDENTS. I SOMETIMES AM ABLE TO SIT AND TALK ABOUT DAY-TO-DAY LIFE WITH RESIDENTS, EVEN THOSE WITH DEMENTIA. IT BRINGS LAUGHTER, SOMETIMES TEARS. ALWAYS A HUG.

I AM GRATEFUL FOR WHAT I HAVE AND FOR WHAT I HAVE TO GIVE TO RESIDENTS. THAT SHARED EXPERIENCE IS VERY IMPORTANT AND IT'S NOT VALUED. IT'S JUST WORK, WORK, WORK.

THERE ARE OFTEN TIMES WHEN WE ARE SHORT-STAFFED. BUT THE WORK HAS TO BE DONE. WE DON'T HAVE THE WORKERS WE NEED AND IT CAUSES MENTAL STRAIN.

I DON'T GET PAID ENOUGH TO WORK SHORT-STAFFED!

MY RESEARCH TELLS ME ABOUT 80 PERCENT OF SHIFTS IN CARE HOMES AND HOME CARE ARE NOT FULLY STAFFED.

106

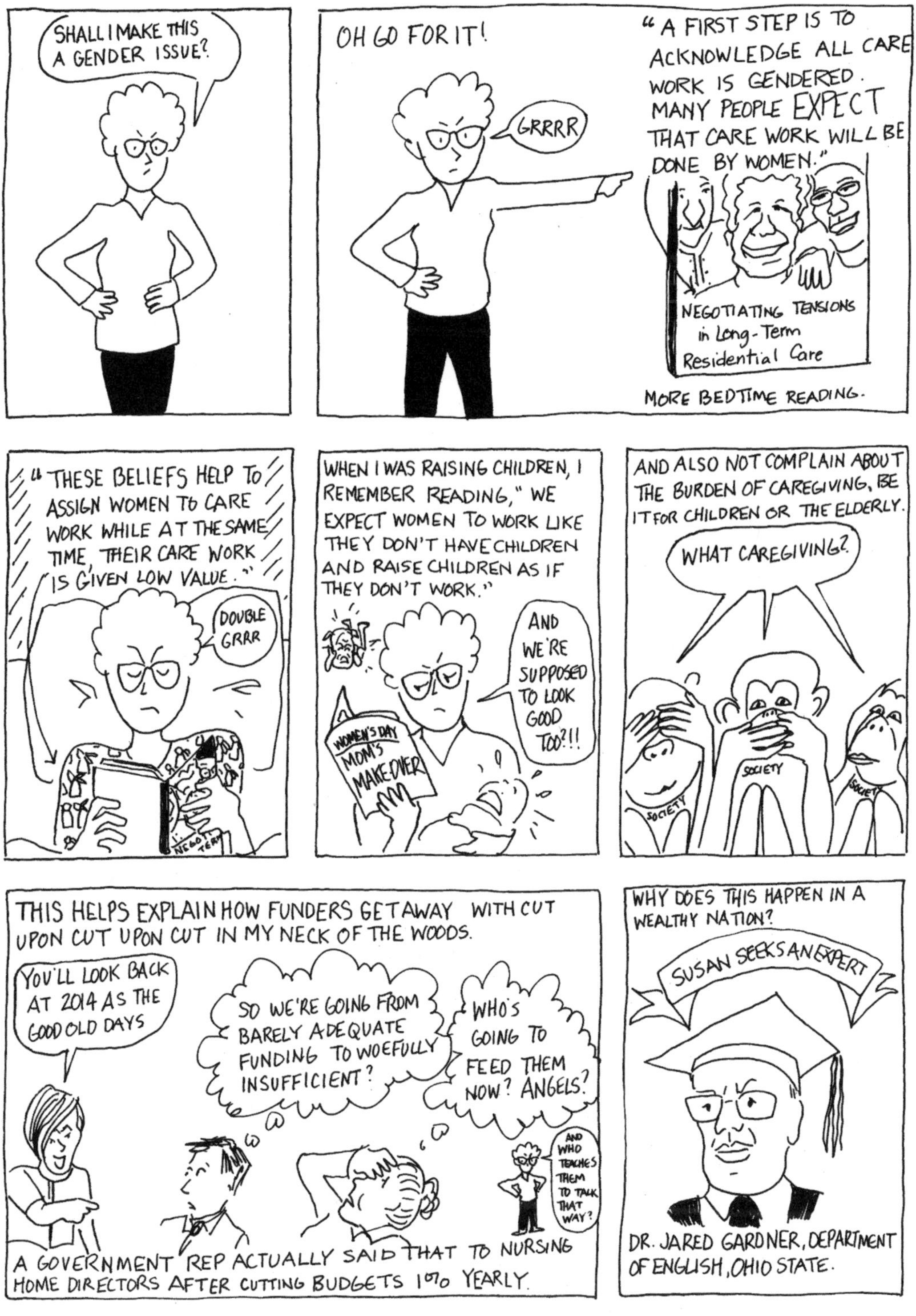
SHALL I MAKE THIS A GENDER ISSUE?
OH GO FOR IT!
GRRRR
"A FIRST STEP IS TO ACKNOWLEDGE ALL CARE WORK IS GENDERED. MANY PEOPLE EXPECT THAT CARE WORK WILL BE DONE BY WOMEN."
NEGOTIATING TENSIONS in Long-Term Residential Care
MORE BEDTIME READING.
"THESE BELIEFS HELP TO ASSIGN WOMEN TO CARE WORK WHILE AT THE SAME TIME, THEIR CARE WORK IS GIVEN LOW VALUE."
DOUBLE GRRR
WHEN I WAS RAISING CHILDREN, I REMEMBER READING," WE EXPECT WOMEN TO WORK LIKE THEY DON'T HAVE CHILDREN AND RAISE CHILDREN AS IF THEY DON'T WORK."
WOMEN'S DAY MOM'S MAKE-OVER
AND WE'RE SUPPOSED TO LOOK GOOD TOO?!!
AND ALSO NOT COMPLAIN ABOUT THE BURDEN OF CAREGIVING, BE IT FOR CHILDREN OR THE ELDERLY.
WHAT CAREGIVING?
SOCIETY
SOCIETY
SOCIETY
THIS HELPS EXPLAIN HOW FUNDERS GET AWAY WITH CUT UPON CUT UPON CUT IN MY NECK OF THE WOODS.
YOU'LL LOOK BACK AT 2014 AS THE GOOD OLD DAYS
SO WE'RE GOING FROM BARELY ADEQUATE FUNDING TO WOEFULLY INSUFFICIENT?
WHO'S GOING TO FEED THEM NOW? ANGELS?
AND WHO TEACHES THEM TO TALK THAT WAY?
A GOVERNMENT REP ACTUALLY SAID THAT TO NURSING HOME DIRECTORS AFTER CUTTING BUDGETS 1% YEARLY.
WHY DOES THIS HAPPEN IN A WEALTHY NATION?
SUSAN SEEKS AN EXPERT
DR. JARED GARDNER, DEPARTMENT OF ENGLISH, OHIO STATE.

HE STUDIES TIME, MONEY AND COMPASSION.

YOU USE THE TERM "CAPITALIST CLOCK." WHAT DOES IT MEAN AND WHAT DOES IT MEAN FOR CAREGIVERS?

IT MEANS EVERYONE HAS TO BE ON THE SAME SHARED MEASUREMENT OF TIME SO THAT TIME CAN BE LINKED TO A VALUE OF MONEY.

THE ILL AND ELDERLY ARE SUNDERED FROM CLOCK TIME YET. IN THE SAME SPACE CLINICIANS ARE BURDENED BY IT.

IT'S TIME TO SPEAK UP. I'LL WRITE A BOOK!

BUT OTHERS HAVE BEEN WRITING ABOUT CAREGIVING ISSUES FOR A WHILE.

SUSAN SEEKS AN EXPERT

JOHN IBBITSON, COLUMNIST, GLOBE AND MAIL, WROTE THE FOLLOWING IN HIS PIECE, "IN THIS AGING SOCIETY, CANADA NEEDS MORE FEMALE LEADERS."

"IMAGINE A MEETING BETWEEN A PRIME MINISTER AND A FINANCE MINISTER, BOTH MEN, AROUND BUDGET TIME."

"IF THE CHOICE IS BETWEEN REPLACING AGING FRIGATES OR INCREASING HOME CARE FUNDING..."

"... THE MEN MAY INCLINE TOWARD THE NAVY, KNOWING THEIR WIVES OR SISTERS WILL MAKE SURE MOM AND DAD ARE LOOKED AFTER."

TRIPLE GRRR

"BUT IF THE LEADERS ARE WOMEN WHO ARE DEALING WITH THEIR OWN AGING PARENTS, MAYBE INCREASED FUNDING FOR PERSONAL SUPPORT WORKERS WOULD TAKE PRIORITY."

HOME CARE APPROVED
HOME CARE APPROVED

HE QUOTES CHI NGUYEN, DIRECTOR OF SOCIAL INNOVATION CANADA.

WE ARE NOT VALUING THIS INCREDIBLY DIFFICULT AND IMPORTANT WORK AND THE KIND OF EMOTIONAL SENSITIVITY TO DO THAT WORK COMPETENTLY.

TAP
TAP TAP
TAP
TAP

SOLUTION SUSAN STRIKES

THERE WASN'T MUCH I COULD DO ABOUT THE TRADITIONAL PATRIARCHAL STATUS QUO. SO I RALLIED ENOUGH TO JOIN THE HOME'S FAMILY COUNCIL.

SIGN UP!

OTHER DAUGHTERS WERE THERE TOO. IN MY MIND I TOOK TO CALLING US THE...

DAUGHTERS OF THE NEAR DEAD

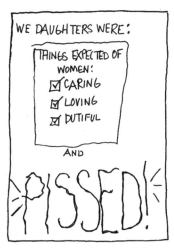

WE DAUGHTERS WERE:

THINGS EXPECTED OF WOMEN:
☑ CARING
☑ LOVING
☑ DUTIFUL

AND

PISSED!

A DAUGHTER ONCE CAME TO SPEAK TO THE FAMILY COUNCIL. SHE WAS GETTING THE RUN-AROUND, MUCH AS I HAD, ABOUT THE CALL BELL.

THE SOCIAL WORKER MOSTLY STARED BLANKLY. SHE SEEMED TO SIMPLY WANT THE DAY OVER. SHE HAD NO ANSWER.

LET'S JUST GIVE THEM ALL DEATH PILLS THEN!!

IT SEEMED THE PROBLEMS IN THE HOME AND THE SYSTEM SPRUNG FROM ECONOMIC, SOCIETAL AND CULTURAL FORCES LARGER THAN FAMILY COUNCIL!

FAMILY COUNCIL AGENDA
1. BATH LIFTS
2. RESIDENT TRANSFER TO HOSPITAL
3. SMASH THE PATRIARCHY!

SOLUTION SUSAN STRIKES AGAIN.

I STILL WANTED TO DO SOMETHING TO HELP.

A BROCHURE WILL DO THE TRICK!

EASY FOR ME TO DO, TOO.

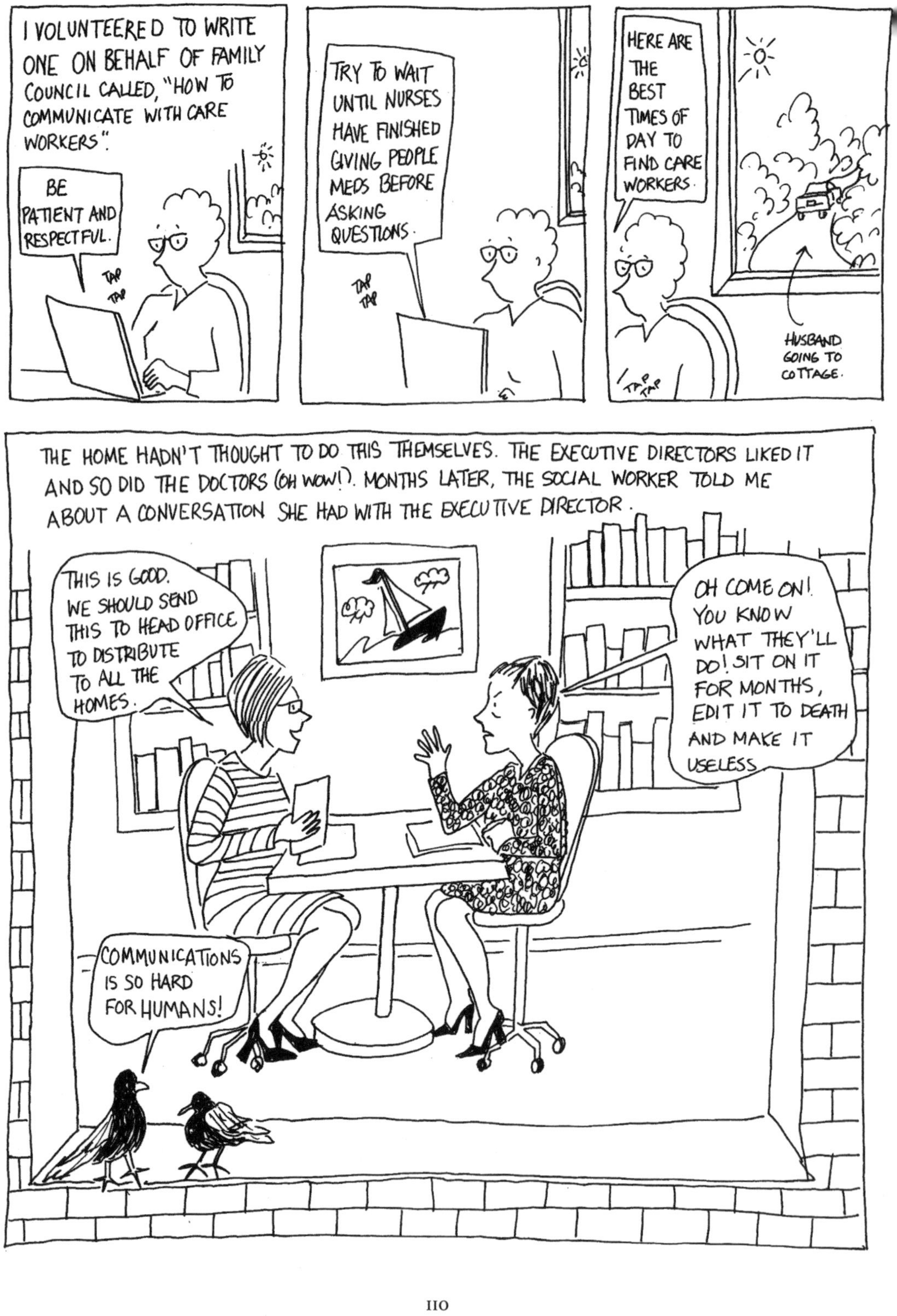
I VOLUNTEERED TO WRITE ONE ON BEHALF OF FAMILY COUNCIL CALLED, "HOW TO COMMUNICATE WITH CARE WORKERS".
BE PATIENT AND RESPECTFUL.
TAP TAP
TRY TO WAIT UNTIL NURSES HAVE FINISHED GIVING PEOPLE MEDS BEFORE ASKING QUESTIONS.
TAP TAP
HERE ARE THE BEST TIMES OF DAY TO FIND CARE WORKERS.
TAP TAP
HUSBAND GOING TO COTTAGE.
THE HOME HADN'T THOUGHT TO DO THIS THEMSELVES. THE EXECUTIVE DIRECTORS LIKED IT AND SO DID THE DOCTORS (OH WOW!). MONTHS LATER, THE SOCIAL WORKER TOLD ME ABOUT A CONVERSATION SHE HAD WITH THE EXECUTIVE DIRECTOR.
THIS IS GOOD. WE SHOULD SEND THIS TO HEAD OFFICE TO DISTRIBUTE TO ALL THE HOMES.
OH COME ON! YOU KNOW WHAT THEY'LL DO! SIT ON IT FOR MONTHS, EDIT IT TO DEATH AND MAKE IT USELESS.
COMMUNICATIONS IS SO HARD FOR HUMANS!

TIME AGAIN FOR
SYSTEMS THAT MAKE HUMANS INHUMANE

IF **PATIENT-CENTERED CARE** IS IMPORTANT TO PATIENT OUTCOMES, WHY IS SUPPORT FOR THE CARE WORKERS **CENTERED ON THE PATIENT** MADE THE LEAST IMPORTANT PRIORITY?

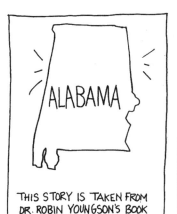

ALABAMA

THIS STORY IS TAKEN FROM DR. ROBIN YOUNGSON'S BOOK "TIME TO CARE".

A CHIEF NURSING OFFICER ASKED STAFF TO CHECK ON EACH RESIDENT ONCE EVERY HOUR ON TOP OF THEIR OTHER DUTIES.

ASK THEM ABOUT PAIN, BATHROOM NEEDS, COMFORT — JUST ASK IF THEY NEED ANYTHING.

OUTCRY! OUTCRY! OUTCRY!

BUT SHE PERSISTED.

LET'S JUST MAKE IT A TRIAL!

WHAT HAPPENED? THE CALL BELLS FELL SILENT.

BUZZ BUZZ BUZZ

NURSES WERE INTERRUPTED LESS AND AN AUDIT SHOWED THEY WALKED A MILE LESS EACH SHIFT.

THEY ALSO SPENT MORE TIME ON DIRECT PATIENT CARE.

AND THE NUMBERS?

PATIENT FALLS:
• REDUCED BY 58%
BED SORES:
• REDUCED BY 39%

!

OF COURSE, THE QUALITY OF "RELATIONAL CARE" BETWEEN THE CARE WORKER AND THE PATIENT — ENGAGING IN PLEASANT CONVERSATION, SPENDING TIME - ISN'T MEASURED.

I WONDERED:
WHAT IF MY BROTHER HAD ASKED REGULARLY WHAT MOM NEEDED?

WHAT IF HE HAD PAID ATTENTION?

WOULD SIBLING SATISFACTION INCREASE?

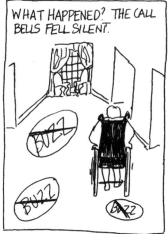

THE QUALITY OF RELATIONAL CARE AMONG SIBLINGS IS MEASURED.

FACT: ONE SIBLING HAS ALL THE PARENTAL RESPONSIBILITY IN 42% OF FAMILIES.

AROUND 44% OF FAMILY CAREGIVERS SAID RELATIONSHIPS WITH THEIR SIBLINGS HAVE DETERIORATED DUE TO THEIR UNWILLINGNESS TO HELP OUT.

ABOUT 25% OF FAMILY CAREGIVERS SAY THEY'D LIKE TO ENCOURAGE THEIR SIBLINGS TO HELP MORE.

SOS

I ONLY FELT MY BROTHER IGNORED ME IN A PASSIVE-AGGRESSIVE WAY. THERE WERE WORSE SIBLINGS.

MY BROTHER COMES HOME AND TELLS ME WHAT TO DO! AND HE DOESN'T HAVE A CLUE!

NOW THAT MOM'S IN A HOME, MY BROTHER WON'T LET ME SELL THE HOUSE. HE WANTS US TO BUY IT BUT NEITHER OF US CAN AFFORD IT!

IT MAKES MONEY REALLY TIGHT FOR US.

MY BROTHER IS OPENLY DISRESPECTFUL TO MY PARENTS, BELITTLING THEM, SCOFFING AT THEM! AND HE SEES THEM MORE OFTEN THAN I DO!

ON THE OTHER EXTREME...

THESE ARE PHOTOS OF THE ALL-EXPENSE TRIP TO AUSTRALIA MY BROTHER TOOK ME ON AS THANKS FOR LOOKING AFTER MOM!

I FOUND A RANGE OF SIBLING EXPERIENCES. MOST WERE FRAUGHT.

PERHAPS I JUST NEEDED TO GET SOME ADULT PERSPECTIVE AND LOOK AT THE WHOLE PICTURE.

NOOOOOOOOOOOO!

CHAPTER NINE

GOING SOUTH FAST

I LONGED FOR CALM, PATIENCE, INNER STRENGTH, AND MATURITY. WHATEVER LITTLE OF THOSE QUALITIES I HAD WAS ERODING.

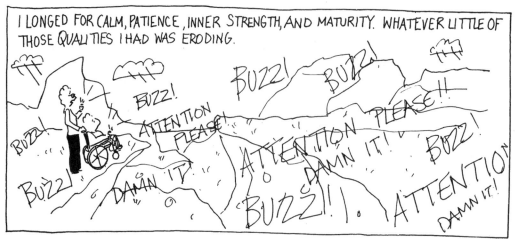

NO ONE SEEMED TO HEAR ME! EVERY APRIL I BOOKED THE HOME'S PARTY ROOM FOR MOM'S BIRTHDAY AND ORDERED BEVERAGES.

I INVITED MY COUSINS WHO WERE SO KIND AS TO DRIVE IN FROM THEIR TOWNS AS WELL AS MOM'S MINISTER AND A FEW CHURCH FRIENDS. MY CLOSE FRIENDS OFTEN CAME TOO. AND EVERY SINGLE YEAR . . .

SO SORRY, YOUR MOM'S NOT READY, AND THE ROOM'S IN USE BY STAFF.

NOTHING FOR YOU HERE IN THE COMMUNICATIONS BOOK.

BUT I SUBMITTED THE FORM TWO WEEKS AGO AS ASKED!

OH! THE COMMUNICATIONS BOOK!

THIS "COMMUNICATIONS" BOOK WAS MEANT TO RECORD THE DAY'S "SOFT" INFORMATION ABOUT EACH RESIDENT - WITH THIS MUCH SPACE FOR EACH PERSON.

WEEK OF APRIL 10

THINGS WERE WRITTEN THERE BUT RARELY READ AT SHIFT CHANGE. HAND WRITING WAS OFTEN POOR.

MISSED APPOINTMENTS, VISITS, OUTINGS, DELIVERIES, PARTIES . . . HAPPENS ALL THE TIME. IT'S JUST NOT READ.

STAFF ARE TOO BUSY!

NURSING DIRECTOR

COMMUNICATIONS BOOK FOR RESIDENTS:
1. READ EVERY SHIFT CHANGE.
2. CARED ABOUT.
3. ACTED UPON.

OR LET'S JUST GIVE THEM DEATH PILLS!

IN THE FACE OF ALL THIS, MY BROTHER WAS THE PERSON I FELT SHOULD REALLY BE ON MY SIDE, SHOULD LISTEN, SHOULD PAY ATTENTION.

I REMEMBER EXACTLY WHEN I DECIDED TO BE RESENTFUL TOWARD MY BROTHER. CHRISTMAS TIME.

THERE WAS EXTRA WORK AT THAT TIME; DECORATING HER ROOM, WRITING CARDS FOR HER, JOINING HER AT THE HOME'S SEASONAL SHOWS, BUYING GIFTS FOR HER TO GIVE TO SPECIAL STAFF AND BUYING MY GIFTS TO HER.

I DIDN'T EXPRESS MY ANGER TO HIM DIRECTLY. INSTEAD…

FOR SOME REASON, RESENTFUL FELT JUST RIGHT.

I REMEMBER IT BEING A CONSCIOUS DECISION.

BUT I DID GET AN ADVENTURE. LOOKING BACK, I MAY HAVE HAD OTHER REASONS FOR RESENTING MY BROTHER THAT I DIDN'T REALIZE.

JUST WHAT IS BURIED BENEATH THE STORIES WE TELL OURSELVES AND EACH OTHER?

MAYBE I WANTED TO KNOW...

WHAT WAS BEHIND MY BROTHER'S SEEMING INDIFFERENCE TO ME?

WHAT WAS BEHIND MY STRONG NEED TO FEEL SEEN, HEARD AND EVEN LOVED BY HIM?

I FELT I HAD TIP-TOED AROUND ENOUGH.

SOLUTION SUSAN STRIKES

I'LL TALK TO HIM DIRECTLY ABOUT MY NEEDS!

BE A GROWN-UP!

I ARRANGED A SKYPE CALL.

THE DAY OF THE CALL I HAD BEEN BUSY RUNNING ERRANDS FOR MOM. I MADE THE CALL, AFTER DROPPING THINGS OFF, DURING HER SUPPER.

SAY HI!

WITH EVERONE IN THE DINING ROOM, THE HALLWAY WAS EMPTY. I SAT AT THE END AND TALKED.

WHEN MOM IS ILL, I FIND IT VERY DIFFICULT. IT'S HARD ENOUGH DAY-TO-DAY.

PLEASE SEND MOM CARDS. SHOW HER YOU CARE.

PLEASE THROW ME A BONE, ACKNOWLEDGE THE BURDEN.

I THOUGHT I WAS REASONABLE, CALM, HONEST.

PLEASE PICK UP MORE OF THE VISITOR'S COST. I HAVE THE DAILY GRIND AND MORE THAN HALF THE FINANCIAL BURDEN. NOT FAIR.

YOU SEEM TO MAKE ASSUMPTIONS ABOUT WHAT I CAN WITHSTAND IN REGARD TO MOM'S CARE

I NEED TO EXPRESS MY FEELINGS TO YOU. THEY HAVE VALIDITY.

HE DIDN'T SAY MUCH. NODDED. LOOKED SURPRISED. HE AGREED I HAD A RIGHT TO MY FEELINGS. HE WOULD SEE IF HE COULD PAY MORE.

I DO LOVE YOU.

HOW'S THE WEATHER?

TO ME, IT WENT WELL.

WRONG!

A MONTH LATER HE REPLIED BY EMAIL IN ANGER, WITH ACCUSATIONS.

FINALLY ATTENTION!

WHAT WAS I EXPECTING? COMPASSION? VALIDATION?

I'D BEEN TOLD.

I HATE BEING TOLD.

BECAUSE I WAS WRONG IN A FUNDAMENTAL WAY.

OH.

GOOGLE
EXPECTATIONS
EXPECTATIONS ARE PREMEDITATED RESENTMENTS.

I WISH I'D FULLY UNDERSTOOD THAT AT THE TIME.

I CONSIDERED REPLYING.

I REFRAINED FROM SENDING IT. (SOME ADULTHOOD RESURFACING.)

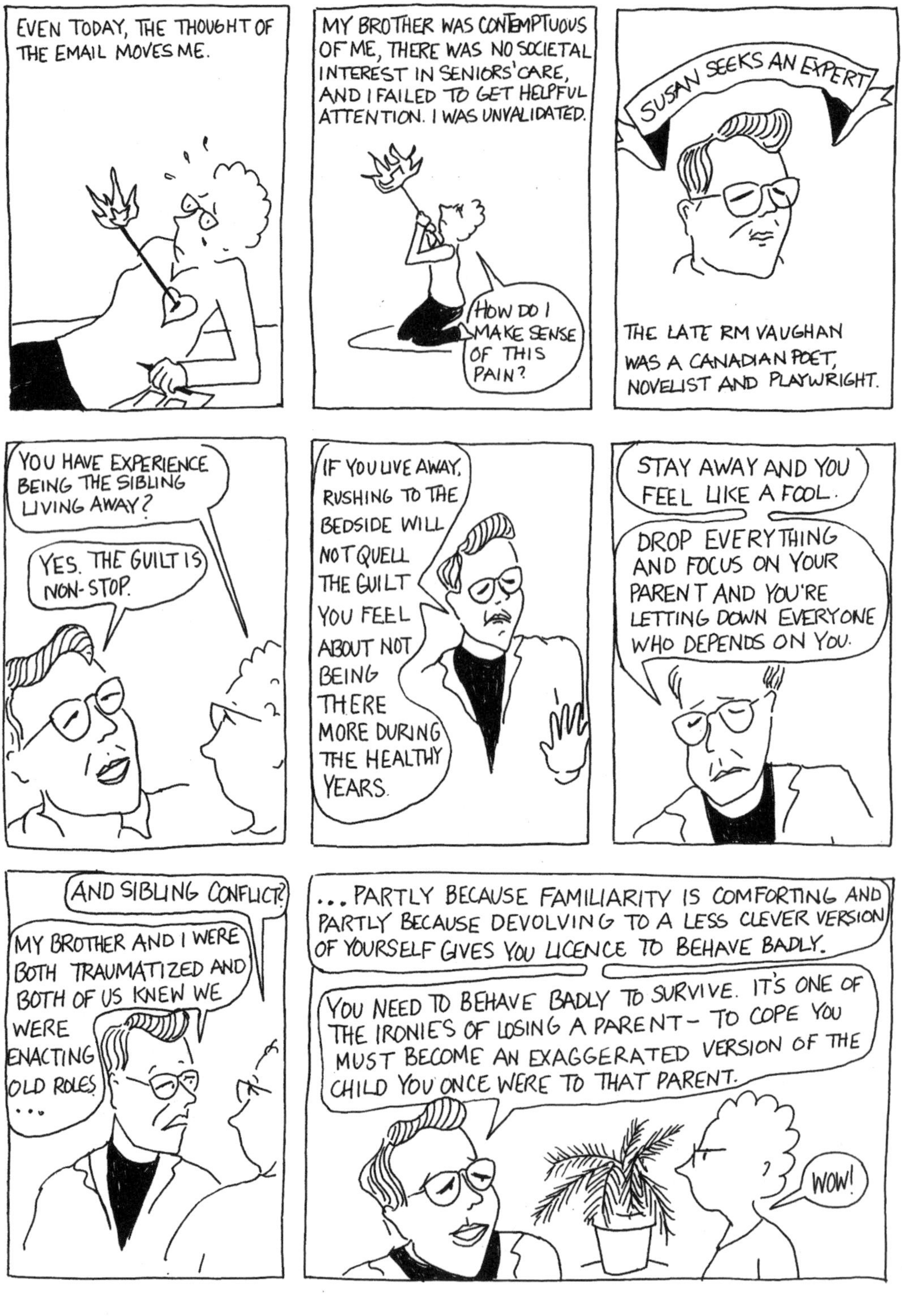
EVEN TODAY, THE THOUGHT OF THE EMAIL MOVES ME.
MY BROTHER WAS CONTEMPTUOUS OF ME, THERE WAS NO SOCIETAL INTEREST IN SENIORS' CARE, AND I FAILED TO GET HELPFUL ATTENTION. I WAS UNVALIDATED.
HOW DO I MAKE SENSE OF THIS PAIN?
SUSAN SEEKS AN EXPERT
THE LATE RM VAUGHAN WAS A CANADIAN POET, NOVELIST AND PLAYWRIGHT.
YOU HAVE EXPERIENCE BEING THE SIBLING LIVING AWAY?
YES. THE GUILT IS NON-STOP.
IF YOU LIVE AWAY, RUSHING TO THE BEDSIDE WILL NOT QUELL THE GUILT YOU FEEL ABOUT NOT BEING THERE MORE DURING THE HEALTHY YEARS.
STAY AWAY AND YOU FEEL LIKE A FOOL.
DROP EVERYTHING AND FOCUS ON YOUR PARENT AND YOU'RE LETTING DOWN EVERYONE WHO DEPENDS ON YOU.
AND SIBLING CONFLICT?
MY BROTHER AND I WERE BOTH TRAUMATIZED AND BOTH OF US KNEW WE WERE ENACTING OLD ROLES...
...PARTLY BECAUSE FAMILIARITY IS COMFORTING AND PARTLY BECAUSE DEVOLVING TO A LESS CLEVER VERSION OF YOURSELF GIVES YOU LICENCE TO BEHAVE BADLY.
YOU NEED TO BEHAVE BADLY TO SURVIVE. IT'S ONE OF THE IRONIES OF LOSING A PARENT - TO COPE YOU MUST BECOME AN EXAGGERATED VERSION OF THE CHILD YOU ONCE WERE TO THAT PARENT.
WOW!

IF I LOOK HONESTLY DEEP INTO MY DARK RECESSES...

... I CAN NOW SEE A PRIMAL NEED TO BE SUPERIOR TO MY BROTHER.

NO.1 CHILD

THIS IS CERTAINLY A HOLD-OVER FROM CHILDHOOD. I DID BETTER IN SCHOOL THAN HE. THIS ALONE PROVED TO ME HE NEEDN'T HAVE BEEN BORN.

DEAN'S LIST

IF MORE THAN HARD EVIDENCE WAS REQUIRED, ONCE I OVERHEARD MY FATHER SAY...

SUSAN'S SMARTER THAN YOU.

I DON'T KNOW WHAT THAT FELT LIKE TO A YOUNG BOY.

I WAS SO SHY, INSECURE AND FELT SO INADEQUATE GROWING UP, HE WAS THE ONE PERSON I COULD FEEL BETTER THAN.

HMMM. JUST NOT AS SATISFYING AS BEATING UP MY BROTHER.

TO THIS DAY IT GALLS ME IF I FEEL HE IS CONDESCENDING TO ME.

IT'S MY JOB TO BE CONDESCENDING TO YOU!

STICK TO THE SCRIPT!

DISTURBED BY THE ANGER IN HIS EMAIL, I SHOWED IT TO FRIENDS FOR COMFORT AND COLLUSION, OF COURSE.

WOW! IT'S ALL ABOUT HIM. DO YOU REALLY WANT A RELATIONSHIP WITH HIM?

WELL... YES.

AT THAT TIME, I DID.

YOU TWO SEEM ENMESHED.

HUH?

MY NURSE FRIEND.

YOU'RE BOTH INTENSELY REACTIVE. YOU HAVEN'T REALLY SEPARATED FROM EACH OTHER AS INDIVIDUALS.

MY HUSBAND WAS LESS ACADEMIC.

HE MIGHT BE RESENTFUL OF YOU PUSHING HIM, THINKING, "SHE DOESN'T LIKE ME ANYWAY." I'M NOT EXCUSING HIM, BUT HE KNOWS YOU DON'T RESPECT HIM.

AND CONTRARY TO MY NURSE FRIEND...

I BET HE DOESN'T EVEN THINK OF YOU MUCH WHEN HE'S NOT HERE.

MAYBE IT'S JUST THAT I HAVEN'T SEPARATED FROM HIM?

WHAT I HAD WANTED WAS VALIDATION FOR THE TOUGH ROLE I HAD WITH MOM. HIS EMAIL WAS A WAKE-UP CALL.

OUCH

BOOM!

IT UPSETS ME EVEN NOW.

I BEGAN TO SEE THE PART I PLAYED IN OUR BROKEN RELATIONSHIP. NOBODY BEAT ME UP AS A KID.

OWW!!

HE NEVER RETALIATED.

BUT WE WEREN'T SPECIAL.

SUSAN SEEKS AN EXPERT

DR. FRANCINE RUSSO WROTE, "THEY'RE YOUR PARENTS TOO!: HOW SIBLINGS CAN SURVIVE THEIR PARENTS' AGING WITHOUT DRIVING EACH OTHER CRAZY."

DR. RUSSO, WHY DO YOU THINK ADULT SIBLINGS HAVE CONFLICT AS PARENTS AGE?

WELL, ALL THE UNMET NEEDS RESURFACE – TO BE LOVED, TO BE APPROVED OF, AND TO BE FINALLY JUDGED AS IMPORTANT OR AS SMART AS YOUR SIBLING.

AS ADULT SIBLINGS, IF TENSIONS ARE TOO HIGH, GET A PROFESSIONAL... EARLY!

SO I DID! THE NEXT TIME HE CAME TO TOWN..

WE NEED TO TALK TO A NEUTRAL THIRD.

HOW ABOUT A LONG WALK TOGETHER INSTEAD?

OK

GIVEN YOUR ANGER, I'D FEEL SAFER WITH A THERAPIST.

I PAID FOR THE THERAPY SESSION. I GOT MORE THAN I BARGAINED FOR.

LOOKING BACK, I WONDERED WHY I PERSISTED. IN PART, IT WAS EMOTIONALLY DIFFICULT TO ACCEPT HOW MUCH HE DISLIKED ME.

OUCH

I ALSO PERSISTED BECAUSE IT WAS MY CONVICTION THERE'S ALWAYS A WAY FORWARD WITH GOOD, HONEST COMMUNICATION.

SOLUTION SUSAN STRIKES

I KNOW! LET'S TALK TO EACH OTHER!

STILL NAIVE.

THE SESSION BEGAN AMICABLY WITH NERVOUS PLEASANTRIES. I FELT DIZZY.

FINALLY I GOT TO THE CRUX OF THE MATTER.

I ASK AND ASK YOU FOR HELP AND ATTENTION YET ALMOST NOTHING CHANGES.

I FEEL AS IF I'M KNOCKING ON A GLASS CEILING

THAT'S EVOCATIVE IMAGERY. WHAT DO YOU SAY TO THAT?

HE DIDN'T HAVE MUCH TO SAY...

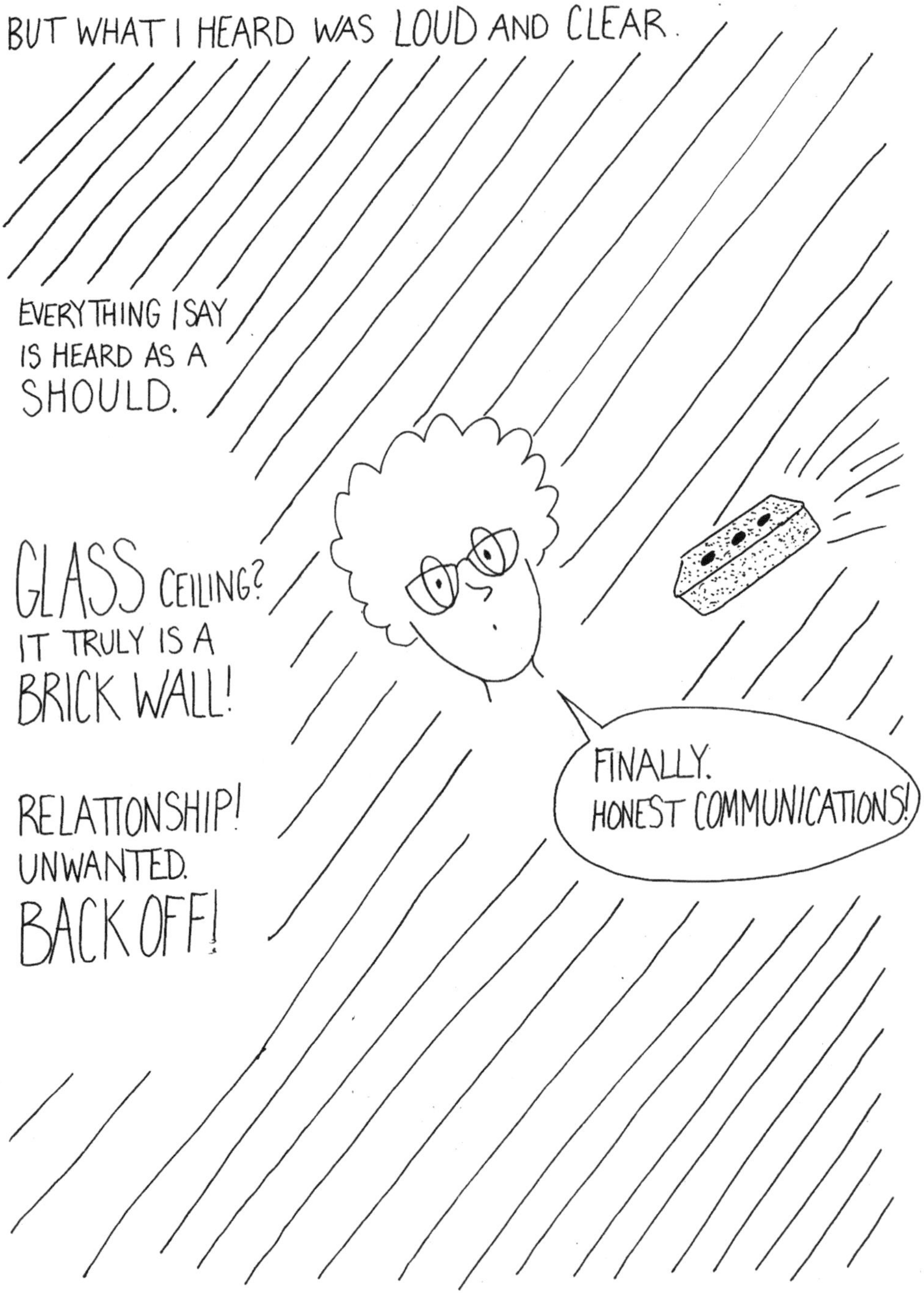
BUT WHAT I HEARD WAS LOUD AND CLEAR.
EVERYTHING I SAY IS HEARD AS A SHOULD.
GLASS CEILING? IT TRULY IS A BRICK WALL!
RELATIONSHIP! UNWANTED. BACK OFF!
FINALLY. HONEST COMMUNICATIONS!

ODDLY, FOR ME, THE ROOM SUDDENLY FILLED WITH LIGHT. THE SUN STREAMED BRIGHTLY THROUGH THE WINDOWS WITH A MAGNIFICENT RADIANCE. EVERYTHING FELT VIBRANT, ALIVE AND SPARKLING.

OH HAPPY DAY!

I FELT A RUSH OF UNCONDITIONAL LOVE TOWARD MY BROTHER, A VALIDATION OF A TRUTH FINALLY COMMUNICATED. JUST MAYBE HE DID KNOW HE'D BEEN UNKIND TOWARD ME WHEN MOM AND I NEEDED HIM.

WHEN WE LEFT, I TOOK HIS HAND, STILL AWASH IN A SENSE OF BLISSFULNESS TOWARD HIM AND THE WHOLE WORLD, AS WE WALKED TOWARD OUR CARS.

CHAPTER TEN

TALKING ABOUT FAMILIES...

... BRINGS OUT THE HIGHEST LEVELS OF VULNERABILITY. IT'S SO CLOSE TO THE BONE OF WHO WE LIKE TO THINK WE ARE.

MY TRANSCENDENCE DIDN'T LAST. THE NEXT MORNING I FELT THAT OLD HATRED OF HIM, NOW FUELED BY HURT.

THE FOLLOWING WEEK I RETURNED TO THE THERAPIST. HAD I HEARD CORRECTLY?

YES.

YOU'RE BOTH STILL WOUNDED CHILDREN.

HE DOESN'T WANT A RELATIONSHIP WITH YOU.

HE KNOWS HOW TO PUSH YOUR BUTTONS AND I SEE YOU HAVE ARROGANCE TOWARD HIM.

JUST START TO NOTICE WHEN YOU FEEL TRIGGERED.

AND TAKE CARE OF YOURSELF.

YOU'VE NEVER SEEN HIM AT HIS BEST, HAVE YOU?

NO. I GUESS I HAVEN'T ALLOWED MYSELF TO.

THAT'S A SHAME.

AFTERWARDS, I HAD CONFLICTING EMOTIONS. I BLOCKED HIM ON FACEBOOK. HE DIDN'T WANT A RELATIONSHIP. I DIDN'T WANT A TRIGGER.

I TOOK MY FEELINGS OUT ON MY FAMILY AND FRIENDS.

WHY DID YOU LEAVE AN EMPTY MUSTARD JAR in the fridge??

A TINY NEW THOUGHT WAS BEGINNING TO EMERGE IN MY CONSCIOUSNESS. IS MY DISTRESS AS MUCH ABOUT ME INVALIDATING MYSELF AND ALSO INVALIDATING HIM AS IT IS ABOUT HIM INVALIDATING ME?

UNCOMFORTABLE! AND TOO MANY SYLLABLES!

IF MY BROTHER AND I WEREN'T SIBLINGS, WE MIGHT GET ALONG. WE MIGHT EVEN BE FRIENDS.

FROM MOM, WE BOTH INHERITED A STRONG SENSE OF SOCIAL JUSTICE.

RESPECT FOR DYING TURTLES!

RESPECT FOR DYING OLDIES!

HE IS GENTLE BY NATURE, ENJOYS A GOOD LAUGH AND LOVES HIS CHILDREN. HE DOES EVERYTHING IN HIS POWER TO SUPPORT THEM.

HE DID DO THINGS FOR MOM. HE SIGNED UP FOR PROFESSIONAL DEVELOPMENT COURSES OUT HERE SO HE COULD VISIT MOST SUMMERS. AT LEAST ONCE, HE HIMSELF PAID TO COME OUT.

HE EVEN RAN A FEW ERRANDS FOR MOM WHILE HERE.

HE CONTINUED TO PAY SOME OF MOM'S VISITOR'S COSTS TO THE END, THOUGH HE REALLY DIDN'T WANT TO.

LIVING FAR AWAY IS, I SUPPOSE, A REASON NOT TO BE ENGAGED. AND HIS JOB WAS CHALLENGING.

HE HAD STUFF TO DO.

ONE TIME HE GOT ME A FREELANCE JOB WHERE HE WORKED. HIS ORGANIZATION PAID MY WAY OUT.

THANKS. BUT WHAT'S THIS GOT TO DO WITH MOM?

MAYBE HE MEANT THIS AS A GESTURE OF ACKNOWLEDGEMENT, ATTENTION, APPRECIATION... WE NEVER TALKED ABOUT IT AS SUCH. JUST A JOB.

PERHAPS NOTHING HE DID WOULD HAVE BEEN ENOUGH FOR ME.

YOU'RE NOT THE MOST GENEROUS INTERPRETER OF HIS MOTIVES.

PERHAPS I LONGED FOR WHAT SIMPLY COULD NOT BE GIVEN.

SOS

SUSAN SEEKS AN EXPERT

DR. JEANNE SAFER KNOWS MORE THAN I. SHE'S A NEW YORK PSYCHOTHERAPIST STUDYING SIBLING CONFLICT.

JUST HOW WIDESPREAD IS SIBLING STRIFE?

AROUND 45 PERCENT OF SIBLINGS SUFFER CONFLICT.

THERE'S AN AWFUL LOT OF IT.

THESE ARE SIBLINGS WHO DON'T GET ALONG, WHO DREAD SEEING EACH OTHER...

... THE OPPOSITE OF WHAT WE LONG FOR IN OUR CLOSEST BIOLOGICAL RELATIVES.

BUT THIS IS THE RELATIONSHIP WE FILE AWAY, SOMETHING WE THINK WE DON'T HAVE TO ADDRESS.

I THINK WHAT SCREWS UP SIBLINGS MORE THAN ANYTHING ELSE ARE PARENTS.

IT'S THE SELF-AWARENESS OF THE PARENTS AND THEIR COMING TO TERMS WITH THEIR OWN CONFLICTS, THEIR OWN FAMILY DYNAMICS...

... THAT MAKE THINGS GO WRONG WITH CHILDREN. IT'S THE HIDDEN DIMENSIONS OF FAMILIES.

JUST WHAT IS BURIED BENEATH THE STORIES WE TELL OURSELVES AND EACH OTHER?

I SUPPOSE ONE CAN ASSUME THAT THE NATION'S CITIZENRY IS PERMEATED BY A STRONG SENSE OF SIBLING INJUSTICE. OF COURSE THERE'S NO COURT OF SIBLING REDRESS.

WHO SAYS SIBLINGS HAVE TO SHARE RESPONSIBILITY FOR AGING PARENTS?

WE, THE EXHAUSTED, DO!

BECAUSE I WAS FEELING LONELY AND ISOLATED, I TOOK TO E-MAILING MY COUSINS WHO HAD KNOWN MOM. I UPDATED THEM ON HER DECLINING CONDITION. I HADN'T SEEN SOME OF THEM SINCE I WAS FOUR. AND PERHAPS I WANTED TO SEARCH FOR SOMETHING MEANINGFUL IN THIS SITUATION. THEY WERE OLDER AND HAD GONE THROUGH THE DECLINE AND DEATH OF THEIR PARENTS. THEY WERE KIND, VALIDATING, SYMPATHETIC AND SUPPORTIVE—A CONTRAST TO WHAT I FELT FROM THE NURSING HOME, GOVERNMENT AND MY BROTHER.

SUSAN WHO? OH, THE LITTLE ONE!

I WONDERED ABOUT THE PATRIARCHY ITSELF.

SUSAN SEEKS AN EXPERT

CHRISTINE HUTCHISON IS A REGISTERED MARRIAGE AND FAMILY THERAPIST.

TELL ME ABOUT THE ARTICLE YOU WROTE, "THE PRICE OF UNPAID EMOTIONAL LABOUR?"

IN MY PRACTICE IT SOMETIMES SEEMS LIKE WOMEN ON AVERAGE HAVE A PhD IN EMOTIONAL LABOUR AND MEN ARE TRYING TO PASS THIRD GRADE.

IT'S SO LOPSIDED!

HONESTLY, I DON'T KNOW HOW TO WORK WITH THIS.

AND AS THE UNSPOKEN RULES OF THE PATRIARCHY HAVE IT, MEN ARE NOT EVER ALLOWED TO FEEL INFERIOR AT ANYTHING!

WE'RE ALL IN A BIND!

I SUPPOSE THESE ARE WAYS TO LOOK AT MY CONFUSION. I REMEMBER MOM SAYING TO ME ONCE WHEN I WAS A TEENAGER...

YOUR FATHER DOESN'T SMOKE, DRINK OR FOOL AROUND.

HE DOESN'T HOLD A GRUDGE LIKE I DO.

BUT HE DOESN'T HELP ME MUCH EITHER WITH OUR RESPONSIBILITIES. NOR DOES HE TAKE ANY INITIATIVE.

HIS POSITIVE QUALITIES LIE IN THE ABSENCE OF NEGATIVE ONES.

MAYBE DAD PASSED THIS PASSIVE INATTENTION ON TO MY BROTHER.

REMEMBER SON, IF IT'S EMOTIONALLY DIFFICULT, RUN A MILE (OR GET ANGRY).

YET MY FATHER WAS A KIND MAN.

YES, YOU SHOULD GO ON TO ART SCHOOL IF YOU CAN AFFORD IT, SUSAN

MY MOTHER WAS VITRIOLIC AT THE IDEA.

DAD LOVED MY MOTHER.

AS SOON AS I SAW HER, I KNEW I LOVED HER. I CAN'T EXPLAIN IT.

WHEN MY AUNT GOT CANCER, MOM AND DAD WOULD DRIVE FROM THE CITY, PICK HER UP, TAKE HER BACK TO THE CITY...

...WAIT FOR HER IN TREATMENT, DRIVE HER HOME, THEN DO THE TWO-HOUR DRIVE BACK TO THE CITY. AND THEY HADN'T GOTTEN ALONG WITH HER.

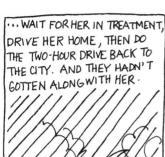

IT WAS THEN I REALIZED WHAT FAMILY MEANT.

MOM WAS KIND TOO. I HAD MAJOR SURGERY IN MY 20's WHEN OUR RELATIONSHIP WAS DISTANT.

I WOKE UP AND WAS SURPRISINGLY GRATEFUL TO FIND HER THERE BESIDE ME.

SHE HAD WAITED FOR HOURS

THAT'S ONE OF THE FEW MEMORIES I HAVE OF MOM SHOWING ME WARMTH AND LOVE. MOSTLY I FELT HER DISAPPROVAL.

♪ LULLABY AND GOOD NIGHT ♪

YOU REALLY CAN'T SING!

SHE WAS BUSINESS-LIKE IN ENSURING WE HAD OPPORTUNITIES. IT WAS A PRACTICAL, EVEN LONELY, KIND OF LOVE. ONCE SHE REFLECTED...

ALWAYS, YOUR DAD AND I ASKED, CAN WE AFFORD IT?

ONE YEAR THE TUITION AT UNIVERSITY WAS RAISED.

WE TOOK ALL OUR SAVINGS SO YOU COULD KEEP GOING.

MARY FRASER KEPT ASKING ME WHY WE DIDN'T GO BACK TO VISIT ENGLAND.

SHE PERSISTED AND FINALLY I SAID, MARY, WE TOOK ALL OUR SAVINGS TO KEEP SUSAN IN SCHOOL!

AND MARY BLUSHED BECAUSE SHE HAD KEPT ON.

MOM NEVER LIKED HER MOTHER. QUEENIE LIVED WITH US WHEN I WAS SIX OR SO. ONE WINTER DAY I SAW MY GENTLE DAD GESTURING IN ANGER BEHIND MY GRANDMOTHER'S BACK.

I LEARNED LATER QUEENIE HAD BEEN SPREADING VICIOUS RUMOURS ABOUT MOM TO THE NEIGHBOURS, SAYING MOM HAD NOT BEEN GIVING HER GOOD CARE. ONE NEIGHBOUR STOPPED TALKING TO MOM. SHE WAS HEARTBROKEN AND ASHAMED. WE MOVED.

MAYBE QUEENIE'S UNKINDNESS HELPS EXPLAIN MOM'S COLDNESS. SHE WAS BITTER ABOUT MY PRE-MARITAL PREGNANCY.

OUR PREMMIE. ♥♥

YOUR BELLY'S DISGUSTING!

IT DIDN'T MATTER THAT OUR RELATIONSHIP WAS SOLID AND I ALREADY HAD A CAREER WITH A GOOD INCOME.

YOU'RE A FOOL!

SHE GAVE ME THE WORST POSSIBLE INSULT...

AND YOU LOOK JUST LIKE QUEENIE!

MY BABY HAD COLIC. ONE EVENING I LEFT HIM WITH HER.

MOM, WHY WAS HE ON THE FLOOR ALONE IN THE DARK CRYING?

WELL, HE WOULDN'T STOP CRYING IN THE CRIB!

WAS SHE LIKE THIS WITH ME WHEN I WAS COLICKY? NONETHELESS, SHE BECAME A LOVING GRANDMOTHER.

EVEN AT OUR WEDDING, SHE DIDN'T APPROVE OF MY HUSBAND.

HARRUMPH! I ALWAYS THOUGHT YOU'D MARRY A LAWYER!

BUT SHE GREW TO LOVE HIM WHEN SHE SAW HOW MUCH HE HELPED WITH DAILY CHORES IN WAYS DAD HADN'T.

DAD HAD A SISTER WITH DOWN'S SYNDROME. TYPICAL FOR THE TIME, SHE WAS PLACED IN AN ASYLUM. SOMEHOW, MOM BECAME HER PRIMARY CAREGIVER EARLY IN THEIR MARRIAGE.

WHENEVER MOM AND DAD VISITED WITH NEW SUPPLIES AND TO SPEND TIME WITH MY AUNT, DAD STAYED IN THE CAR.

SHE'S YOUR SISTER!

YOU SHOULD AT LEAST SAY HELLO!

DECADES LATER, WHEN I WAS WITH MOM IN THE NURSING HOME...

DO YOU THINK YOUR OWN DAD HAD A HAPPY LIFE AFTER WWI?

NO.

BECAUSE OF QUEENIE. SHE WAS MEAN.

HOW?

I DON'T KNOW. SHE HAD A MEAN CHARACTER.

WAS SHE MEAN TO YOU?

YES!

WELL, WE CAN ALL BE MEAN.

BUT WE DON'T ALL HAVE A MEAN CHARACTER.

YOU DON'T, DO YOU MOM?

HA! ONLY YOU CAN ANSWER THAT!

WELL, IT'S ALL IN THE PAST NOW!

MY PSYCHOTHERAPIST AND I TALKED ABOUT THIS INCIDENT.

YOUR MOTHER'S MOTHER KEPT HER UNDER HER THUMB.

MY THERAPIST AT THE TIME HAD WILD EYES AND I WAS SOMETIMES SCARED OF HIM.

YOUR MOTHER MAY HAVE TRIED TO DO THE SAME WITH YOU.

IT'S NOT YOUR BROTHER YOU HATE. IT'S YOUR MOTHER.

THREE WORDS: TRANS. FER. ENCE.*

NO! I LOVE MY MOTHER!

LOOK AT ALL I DO FOR HER!

* TRANSFERENCE: THE REDIRECTION TO A SUBSTITUTE OF EMOTIONS THAT WERE ORIGINALLY FELT IN CHILDHOOD.

I FEEL SHAME FOR BULLYING MY BROTHER. I TRIED TO TALK TO HIM ABOUT THAT ONCE. I FELT THE HAND AGAIN.

DON'T TALK TO ME!

HE SAID HE ONLY REMEMBERED ME DEFENDING HIM IN FRONT OF A NEIGHBOURHOOD BULLY.

BUT I'M YOUR MEAN OLDER SISTER!

DEFLECT

AND I STILL PAY SCANT ATTENTION TO HIS ENVIRONMENTAL WORK.

I DON'T CARE WHAT YOU KNOW UNTIL I KNOW THAT YOU CARE

MAYBE WE COULDN'T COMMUNICATE WITHIN OUR BIRTH FAMILY BECAUSE WE'RE COVERING OUR SHAMEFUL ASSES?

PERHAPS HE AND I CAN'T BE KIND TO ONE ANOTHER BECAUSE WE WEREN'T SHOWN HOW TO LOOK KINDLY AT OUR OWN INNER FEARS AND FLAWS.

I HATE MYSELF.

PERHAPS WE EACH FELT SHAME.

HEY! I'M READY NOW TO BE THE LOVING SISTER YOU NEVER HAD. BUT ONLY IF YOU'LL BE A LOVING BROTHER, OF COURSE.

RIGHT.

JUST BECAUSE I NEEDED A LOVING AND SUPPORTIVE BIRTH FAMILY AS MOM DECLINED DIDN'T MEAN I COULD EXPECT IT - AS IF THERE WERE NO PAST.

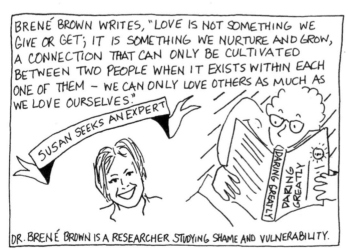

BRENÉ BROWN WRITES, "LOVE IS NOT SOMETHING WE GIVE OR GET; IT IS SOMETHING WE NURTURE AND GROW, A CONNECTION THAT CAN ONLY BE CULTIVATED BETWEEN TWO PEOPLE WHEN IT EXISTS WITHIN EACH ONE OF THEM - WE CAN ONLY LOVE OTHERS AS MUCH AS WE LOVE OURSELVES."

SUSAN SEEKS AN EXPERT

DARING GREATLY

DR. BRENÉ BROWN IS A RESEARCHER STUDYING SHAME AND VULNERABILITY.

WHAT ABOUT THE LONG-TERM CARE SYSTEM? DOES SOCIETY GET AWAY WITH IGNORING AND UNDERFUNDING IT BECAUSE WE DENY THE FACT OF OUR OWN AGING AND DEATH?

YES!

I ONCE WORKED WITH THE GENERAL MEDICINE MANAGER AT THE HOSPITAL. THE UNIT HELD MOSTLY OLDER PEOPLE.

I LOVE THE PATIENTS ON THIS UNIT.

I DIDN'T GET IT.

OH DEAR GOD. IS SHE OUT OF HER MIND??

THOSE OF US WHO WORKED ON THE CONTINUING CARE FILE AT THE DEPARTMENT OF HEALTH WOULD ROUTINELY MOCK THE OLD.

PRETEND WALKER RACE!

NOW THAT I KNOW AND LOVE PEOPLE WITH WALKERS AND WHEELCHAIRS, I'M ASHAMED OF THAT.

I HAD SEVEN BROTHERS, ALL MISERABLE!

I'M GETTING OLDER TOO.

WHO HAS DROOPIER JOWLS, HER OR ME?

OH HER. DEFINITELY!

I FEAR MY OWN DECLINE.

HEART STONE HOME

NO! NOT MOI!

I NOW KNOW THAT MAY DEPEND ON HEALTH ISSUES BEYOND MY CONTROL.

DR. ROBERT BUTLER COINED THE TERM "AGEISM".

IT'S A PROCESS OF SYSTEMATIC STEREOTYPING OF AND DISCRIMINATION AGAINST PEOPLE BECAUSE THEY ARE OLD.

HE WAS AN AMERICAN PHYSICIAN GERONTOLOGIST AND AUTHOR.

AGEISM ALLOWS THE YOUNGER GENERATIONS TO SEE OLDER PEOPLE AS DIFFERENT FROM THEMSELVES.

HE WROTE YOUNG PEOPLE SUBTLY CEASE TO IDENTIFY WITH THEIR ELDERS AS HUMAN BEINGS. I WAS AN AGEIST.

MOVE IT LADY!

MAYBE I STILL AM!

I FOUND IT ALL VERY DIFFICULT. ONE TIME
I TOOK A MONK AND A POET TO BED FOR COMFORT.

* EXCERPT FROM THE CHANT,
"WATERING SEEDS OF JOY"
— THICH NHAT HANH

** EXCERPT FROM THE POEM,
"A PATIENT OLD CRIPPLE"
— JENNY JOSEPH

CHAPTER ELEVEN

STICK AROUND AND OLD WILL FIND YOU

REALLY.

I REMEMBER MOM ALWAYS ASKED ME ABOUT HER APPEARANCE WHEN I WAS A TEENAGER. SHE WAS IN HER 50's.

DO YOU LIKE MY PERM? IT'S SHORTER.

YES.

WHATEVER. IT'S JUST AN OLD PERSON HAIRDO.

OUR HUMAN MINDS ALWAYS SEEK PLEASURE TO DENY THE FACT WE DIE.

PAR-TAY!

YES YOU'LL LIVE FOREVER SUSAN! -YOUR BRAIN

FOR WOMEN, CONSUMERISM - ESPECIALLY FASHION - EXPLOITS THIS INBORN DELUSION.

LIKE MY NEW PERM?

FASHION IS FREE FROM:
· SICKNESS
· SAGGING
· DEATH

IT'S A CURE!

IT'S A BANDAID. WORSE, IT MAKES US ASHAMED OF OURSELVES WHEN WE HAVE NO REASON TO BE. AGING AND DEATH ARE NATURAL AND UNAVOIDABLE.

DESPITE MY NEW PERM, I KEEP AGING!

ME, AT MY HAIRDRESSER'S THESE DAYS ...

I'M NOT READY TO GO GREY YET BUT I DON'T WANT TO BE THAT WOMAN WHO DENIES SHE'S AGING SO COULD YOU JUST PUT FLATTERING HINTS OF PURE SILVER THROUGHOUT AND GIVE ME A VERY YOUTHFUL CUT?

I DON'T WANT TO LEAVE HERE LOOKING MY AGE!

IT'S NATURAL TO FEAR DEATH. BUT WAS IT SMART TO BUILD ENTIRE SOCIAL SYSTEMS AROUND IT?

BUY SO YOU WON'T DIE!

EARLY ECONOMIST.

OUR ECONOMY AND SOCIETY EVOLVED TO PLACE MORE AND MORE VALUE ON INDIVIDUALISM AND COMPETITION, SELF-INTEREST AND SELF-RELIANCE. TO LIVE IS TO WORK, TO CONSUME. I FIND MYSELF BELIEVING THAT AT A VISERAL LEVEL.

IT DOESN'T WORK, SUSAN.

NO. IT DOESN'T.

THERE'S ALMOST A MORAL EXPECTATION EVERY PERSON SHOULD BE PHYSICALLY AND FINANCIALLY WELL. AND PRODUCTIVE.

BLESS ME FOR I HAVE SHOPPED

AGING IS SEEN AS AN INDIVIDUAL FAILING. THE ULTIMATE FAILURE IS FAILING TO LIVE: DEATH.

OOOF

IF YOU'RE NOT ABLE TO BE PRODUCTIVE, YOU'RE SEEN AS HAVING NO VALUE.

LET'S JUST GIVE MOST OF US DEATH PILLS THEN!

SUSAN SEEKS AN EXPERT TARA HENLEY

AUTHOR, "LEAN OUT: A MEDITATION on the MADNESS of MODERN LIFE."

THE QUESTION HERE IS HOW WILL THE ECONOMY SUPPORT PAYING PEOPLE FOR OFFERING COMPASSIONATE CAREGIVING?

IT WILL TAKE CHANGING THE VALUES OF OUR ECONOMY FROM MAXIMIZING EXCHANGES AND MONEY TO MAXIMIZING THE VALUE OF LIFE.

RIGHT NOW, ECONOMICS PUTS THE ONUS ON INDIVIDUALS TO CHANGE WHEN THEY'RE IN EXPLOITIVE SITUATIONS SUCH AS LOW-PAID BUT IMPORTANT CAREGIVING WORK.

IT ANGERS ME!

IT SEEMS TO ME THAT GOVERNMENTS HAVE DECIDED IT'S SAFE TO UNDERFUND COMPASSIONATE LONG TERM CARE. I CALLED GRAHAM STEELE FROM CHAPTER 5.

HOW DO THEY GET AWAY WITH THAT?

POLITICIANS ARE MOSTLY GOOD PEOPLE. COSTS ARE GOING UP AND THERE'S NO NEW MONEY. THEY'RE OVERWHELMED.

LONG TERM CARE IS NOT CONDUCIVE TO SIMPLE SOLUTIONS THAT MAKE POLITICIANS LOOK GOOD. THAT'S WHY IT'S LOW ON THEIR PRIORITY LIST.

I REMEMBERED A NURSING HOME DIRECTOR SAYING AT BUDGET TIME:

YOU JUST HAVE TO LAUGH OR YOU'LL CRY.

SIGH.

THIS TENSION EXISTS WITHIN LONG TERM CARE ITSELF. I TOLD TWO DIFFERENT PEOPLE THE PREMISE OF THIS BOOK:

A FORMER SENIOR LEADER OF THE HEALTH DEPARTMENT.

PEOPLE ARE GOING OUT OF THEIR MINDS TRYING TO GIVE GOOD CARE IN THIS SYSTEM. YOU'RE WAY TOO NEGATIVE! THESE ARE GOOD FACILITIES!

LIVING IN THEM IS A GOOD EXPERIENCE 90% OF THE TIME. PEOPLE'S HEARTS ARE IN THE RIGHT PLACE.

NURSING HOME RESIDENTS ARE HIGHLY DEPENDENT.

A LOT OF THINGS CAN'T BE FIXED.

A FORMER NURSING HOME EXECUTIVE DIRECTOR.

THE WAY WE TREAT PEOPLE IN NURSING HOMES IS ABOMINABLE! THEY'RE RARELY HUGGED. THEY SHARE BEDROOMS AND DINING ROOM TABLES WITH PEOPLE THEY MIGHT HAVE NOTHING IN COMMON WITH.

WE DON'T ASK WHAT THEY WANT ABOUT HARDLY ANYTHING. IT'S AS IF THEY'VE STOPPED BEING HUMAN. THEY'RE FRAIL, DEPENDENT, YES. BUT THAT MAKES THEM LESS?! NOBODIES!?

THEY'RE BOTH RIGHT: SYSTEM VS. HEART.

ERROR!

A LOT OF PEOPLE HAVE THOUGHT ABOUT THIS BUT LITTLE CHANGES.

THE GREAT SECRET... IS THAT YOU REALLY HAVEN'T CHANGED IN... EIGHTY YEARS. YOUR BODY CHANGES BUT YOU DON'T CHANGE... AND THAT CAUSES CONFUSION.

AUTHOR DORIS LESSING.

IF WE HAD THE COURAGE TO THINK AND REFLECT ABOUT LIFE AND DEATH, WE WOULD RAISE OUR CHILDREN DIFFERENTLY... WE WOULD MAKE DEATH AND DYING A PART OF LIFE AGAIN.

AUTHOR ELISABETH KÜBLER-ROSS.

SYSTEMS THAT MAKE HUMANS INHUMANE

ECONOMIC AND MEDICAL SYSTEMS THAT WAGE BATTLE AGAINST DEATH INSTEAD OF WORKING COMPASSIONATELY TO EASE THE TRANSITION!

THE TRAGEDY OF OLD AGE IS NOT THE FACT THAT EACH OF US MUST GROW OLD AND DIE,

BUT THAT THE PROCESS OF DOING SO HAS BEEN MADE UNNECESSARILY AND AT TIMES EXCRUCIATINGLY PAINFUL, HUMILIATING, DEBILITATING AND ISOLATING.

DR. ROBERT BUTLER

TAKING STOCK, I REALIZE I HAVEN'T USED MY "LOOKING FOR THE POSITIVE" ARROW.

SOLUTION SUSAN STRIKES

I CERTAINLY DID SEE MOMENTS OF COMPASSION IN MOM'S NURSING HOME.

REBECCA, OVER 100, WAS ALMOST UNCONSCIOUS.

BUT EVERY FEW MONTHS SHE'D COME TO FOR A WHILE AND BE LUCID.

HELP! I'M STUCK IN MY CHAIR!

SHE WAS FAR FROM WALKING AND ONLY LEFT HER WHEELCHAIR FOR BED.

I CAN'T GET OUT!

ONE TIME I SAW THE HEAD OF PHYSIOTHERAPY WALK BY AND STOP. EVERYONE ELSE WAS IGNORING HER.

I WANT OUT!

WE CAN'T GET YOU OUT. IT'S ALMOST SUPPER.

HE HELD HER HAND VERY TENDERLY AND GAZED KINDLY AT HER UNTIL SUPPER. SEEING THIS BROKE MY HEART.

GENERALLY, THE WAY THINGS WERE ORGANIZED MADE COMPASSION DIFFICULT, EVEN FOR THE DAUGHTERS OF THE NEAR DEAD.

EXIT

GARDEN VIEW
RMS 1-65

PRINCESS VIEW
RMS 65-130

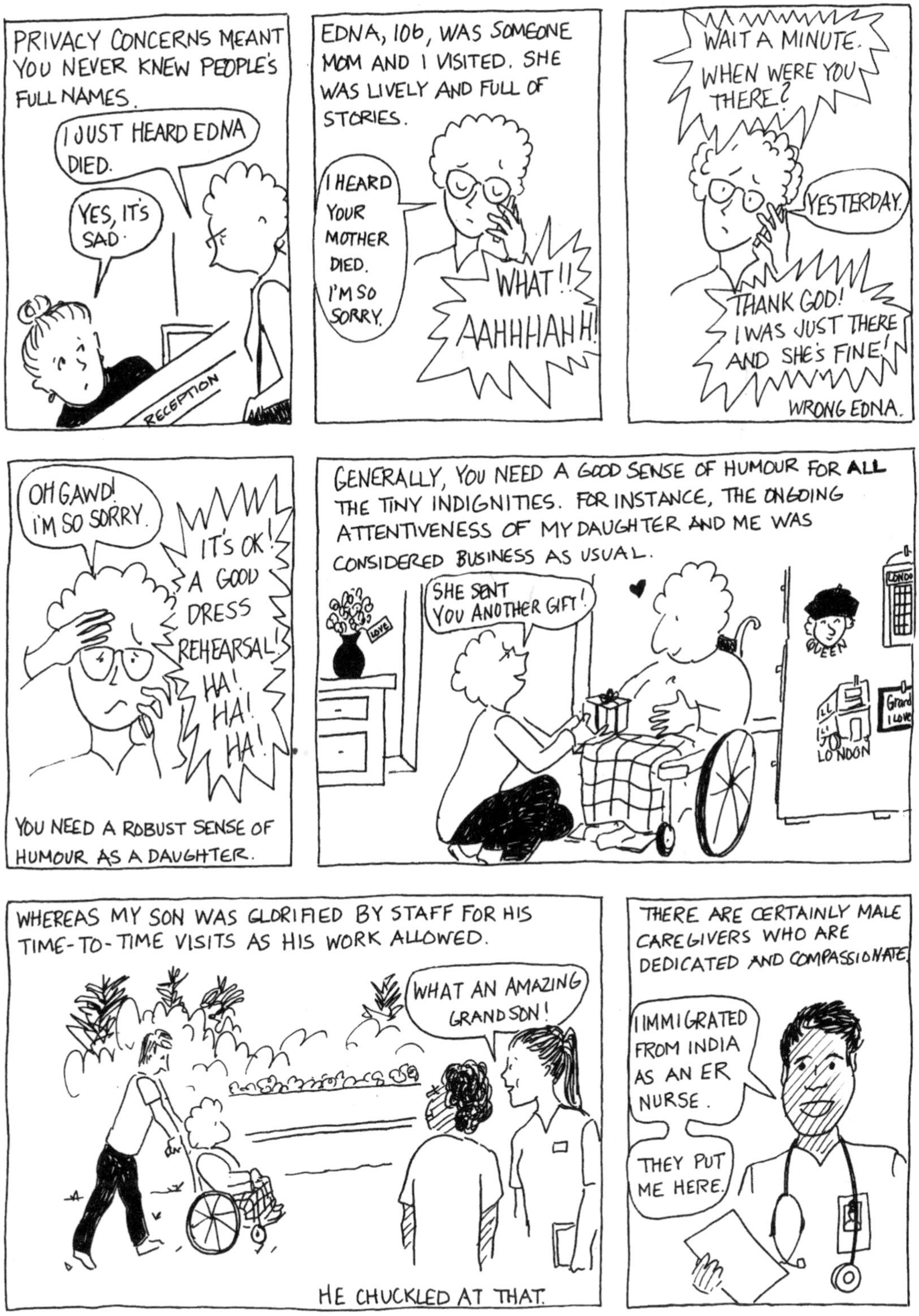
PRIVACY CONCERNS MEANT YOU NEVER KNEW PEOPLE'S FULL NAMES.
I JUST HEARD EDNA DIED.
YES, IT'S SAD.
RECEPTION
EDNA, 106, WAS SOMEONE MOM AND I VISITED. SHE WAS LIVELY AND FULL OF STORIES.
I HEARD YOUR MOTHER DIED. I'M SO SORRY.
WHAT!! AAHHHAHH!
WAIT A MINUTE. WHEN WERE YOU THERE?
YESTERDAY.
THANK GOD! I WAS JUST THERE AND SHE'S FINE!
WRONG EDNA.
OH GAWD! I'M SO SORRY.
IT'S OK! A GOOD DRESS REHEARSAL! HA! HA! HA!
YOU NEED A ROBUST SENSE OF HUMOUR AS A DAUGHTER.
GENERALLY, YOU NEED A GOOD SENSE OF HUMOUR FOR ALL THE TINY INDIGNITIES. FOR INSTANCE, THE ONGOING ATTENTIVENESS OF MY DAUGHTER AND ME WAS CONSIDERED BUSINESS AS USUAL.
SHE SENT YOU ANOTHER GIFT!
LOVE
QUEEN
LONDON
WHEREAS MY SON WAS GLORIFIED BY STAFF FOR HIS TIME-TO-TIME VISITS AS HIS WORK ALLOWED.
WHAT AN AMAZING GRANDSON!
HE CHUCKLED AT THAT.
THERE ARE CERTAINLY MALE CAREGIVERS WHO ARE DEDICATED AND COMPASSIONATE.
I IMMIGRATED FROM INDIA AS AN ER NURSE.
THEY PUT ME HERE.

I STAYED BECAUSE I ENJOY IT. THE MEDICAL ISSUES ARE COMPLEX AND CHALLENGING. I LIKE THE PEOPLE. I LIKE SEEING THEM HOLISTICALLY.

IT'S REWARDING.

FACT:

IN STUDIES OF PHYSICIAN CAREER SATISFACTION, GERIATRICIANS COME OUT ON TOP, DESPITE THE LOW STATUS OF THE SPECIALTY.

THE ORIGINAL HIPPOCRATIC OATH SAYS:

TO CURE WHEN POSSIBLE,

TO HEAL SOMETIMES,

TO CARE ALWAYS.

HE OMITTED "DESERVING OF A LIVING WAGE FOR CARE WORKERS."

SOLUTION SUSAN STRIKES

LET'S ADDRESS AGING WITH COMPASSION! YES WE CAN!

SOLUTION SUSAN

I'M HOLDING THIS NEWS CONFERENCE SO WE CAN COME TOGETHER AND DISCUSS MORE COMPASSIONATE WAYS TO OFFER CARE.

ALL OF US - CARE RECIPIENTS, FAMILY MEMBERS, GOVERNMENT, UNIONS, CARE WORKERS, PRIVATE OWNERS, ECONOMISTS, AND EVERYONE WHO'S AGING— NEED TO DISCUSS HOW TO SERVE PEOPLE WITH COMPASSION IN AN AFFORDABLE WAY . . .

. . . RESPECTFULLY AND WITH DECENT PAY FOR THE CARE WORKERS.

LET'S LISTEN TO EACH OTHER AND WORK TOGETHER OVER TIME.

IT WON'T BE EASY BUT WE CAN DO IT!

WE HUMANS PUT PEOPLE ON THE MOON AFTER ALL!

MY SOLUTIONS ARE NOT ALWAYS REALISTIC.

MAYBE ALL OF THE COMMUNICATIONS PROFESSION IS ABOUT CONTROLLING WHAT PEOPLE HEAR, NOT LISTENING AND EXCHANGING POINTS OF VIEW. IT'S ABOUT POWER. AND APPEARANCES.

I AGREE WITH GERIATRICIAN LOUISE ARONSON...

THE WAY FORWARD?

SIMPLE. JUSTICE IN POLICY, KINDNESS IN ATTITUDE.

DR. ARONSON

SUSAN SEEKS AN EXPERT OR TWO

SIMPLE? SOMETHING'S GETTING IN THE WAY OF JUSTICE AND KINDNESS! WHAT IS IT?

WE'RE IN A WORLD WHERE DEEP CONNECTION IS AVOIDABLE BECAUSE THERE'S SO MUCH CONNECTION WITHOUT MEANING.

IT DOESN'T SERVE PEOPLE WHO ARE DOING WELL TO CARE FOR PEOPLE WHO AREN'T.

AND WE'VE BEEN TRAINED TO RUN AWAY FROM DIFFICULT FEELINGS.

FAILURE OF EMPATHY AND RESPECT ARE CENTRAL.

PAYING ATTENTION IS THE FOUNDATIONAL ACT OF EMPATHY FOR EXPERIENCES OTHER THAN ONE'S OWN.

DR. EMMA KENNY, ENGLISH PSYCHOLOGIST AND REBECCA SOLNIT, AMERICAN WRITER.

WHAT I KNOW IS THAT PAYING ATTENTION WITH TIME AND CARE WAS REWARDING FOR MOM AND ME.

THIS IS MY DAUGHTER. ISN'T SHE AMAZING?!

I HAD NEVER HEARD HER PRIDE IN ME BEFORE.

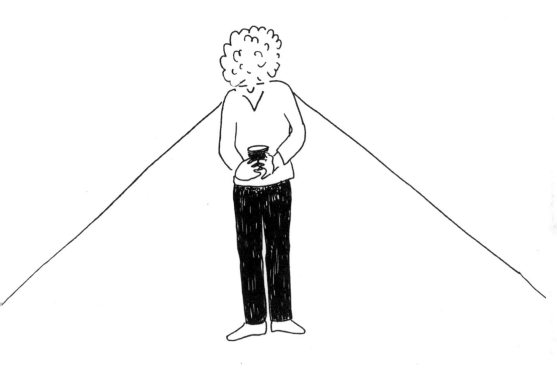

AND THEN
SHE DIED.

CHAPTER TWELVE

NO ONE GETS OUT ALIVE.

BEHOLD ALL YE
WHO DO PASS BY,
AS YE ARE NOW
SO ONCE WAS I.
AS I AM NOW
YE SOON SHALL BE.
PREPARE FOR DEATH
AND FOLLOW ME.

MY FAVOURITE CHILDHOOD HAUNT — THE LOCAL GRAVEYARD FALLING INTO THE SEA.

I'VE BEEN OBSESSED WITH DEATH FOR A LONG TIME. MY DAD WAS THE LOCAL OLD AGE PENSION OFFICER. HE LISTENED TO THE NOON OBITUARIES EVERY DAY WHILE WE KIDS WERE HOME FOR LUNCH. THAT'S HOW HE KNEW TO CUT OFF THE PENSIONS.

WAAAA!

GRRRP

QUIET!

I SAID QUIET!

I'VE PAID ATTENTION TO OBITS EVER SINCE, EVEN AS A TEENAGER.

GOOD. MORE FUEL FOR MY ANGST.

TO THIS DAY, I TEND TO TURN CONVERSATIONS TOWARD DEATH.

A CORPSE'S ARM MUSCLES CONTRACT DURING CREMATION AROUND 670°C.

IT LOOKS AS IF THEY'RE RAISING THEIR FISTS TO BOX.

I REALLY CAN'T BRING ANYONE HOME.

I BECAME LESS ENTHUSIASTIC WHEN DEATH WENT FROM A FASCINATING ABSTRACT NOTION TO MOM'S ACTUAL DYING.

SUSAN, SOMETHING'S VERY WRONG BUT WE'RE NOT GOING TO DO DIAGNOSTIC SURGERY ON A 99 YEAR OLD! YOU WOULDN'T WANT THAT!

OOOOOOHH!

YOU'RE A BIT TOO MATTER-OF-FACT FOR MY LIKING.

AND WHO TEACHES DOCTORS TO TALK THAT WAY?

ALTHOUGH MOST OF US FEAR DEATH, THERE'S SOME PEACE AROUND IT AMONG NURSING HOME RESIDENTS.

PLEASE PASS THE SUGAR.

MY PLEASURE.

MOM'S 106 YEAR OLD FRIEND EDNA...

I DON'T KNOW WHY HE JUST DOESN'T COME AND TAKE ME!

HE MUST BE WAITING FOR ME TO IMPROVE!

HAR! HAR!

HAR! HAR!

HAR!

THE SUMMER BEFORE MOM DIED, MY COUSIN TOOK MOM'S BROTHER HERE TO VISIT. HE WAS 89, FRAIL, BUT BRAVED THE FLIGHT WILLINGLY.

MY COUSIN AND I TOOK THEM OUT TO NICE SPOTS THEY'D REMEMBERED.

I WAS ALWAYS IMPRESSED YOU ROSE TO BE HOSPITAL ADMINISTRATOR.

MOM SHRUGGED.

THEY HAD A GOOD TIME TOGETHER OVER SEVERAL DAYS. THEN...

I DON'T SUPPOSE WE'LL SEE EACH OTHER AGAIN.

NO.

GOODBYE.

GOODBYE.

A SLIGHT SADNESS. NO TEARS. JUST A TURNING AWAY TO WHATEVER CAME NEXT. ANOTHER MEAL. ANOTHER DAY. DEATH.

THE FOLLOWING SPRING, MOM BEGAN SUFFERING ACUTE STOMACH PAIN. SHE BLAMED HERSELF.

I DON'T KNOW WHY I'M BEHAVING SO BADLY.

NO, NO, NO. I DON'T KNOW WHY.

SHE GREW INCREASINGLY VERY SILENT, LESS ENGAGED, AND ATE LESS AND LESS.

EVENTUALLY SHE STOPPED GETTING OUT OF BED. SHE RANG THE CALL BELL A LOT. SHE WRITHED.

SUSAN, SHE RINGS THE CALL BELL ALL THE TIME!

I BEGAN TO FIND THE CALL BELL UNPLUGGED AGAIN.

AND ONCE AGAIN THE WHIRLPOOLS OF WEIRDNESS RESURFACED, ESPECIALLY AROUND COMMUNICATIONS.

HELP!

MOM'S GETTING PAIN MEDS WITH HER RESOURCE DRINK NOW.

I DON'T SEE RESOURCE IN THE ORDER.

MEDS CART

RESOURCE IS A HIGH-NUTRITION DRINK PEOPLE ARE GIVEN WHEN THEY STOP EATING.

BUT STAFF ON OTHER SHIFTS ARE PUTTING HER PAIN MEDS IN HER RESOURCE DRINK.

SHE'S NOT EATING SO CRUSHING THEM IN HER FOOD IS POINTLESS!

MEDS CART

LOOK, I CAN'T DO IT WITHOUT THE ORDER!

MOM, IN PAIN, GOT HER MEDS CRUSHED IN HER MEAL THAT DAY, WHICH SHE DIDN'T EAT.

NEXT DAY...

SUSAN, I JUST SAW THE ORDER. IT WASN'T WHERE I THOUGHT IT'D BE. SORRY.

GRRRRR

WAS IT IN THE COMMUNICATIONS BOOK?

I WAS DEEPLY SADDENED TO SEE MOM SINK INTO CONSTANT PAIN.

AAAAAHHHH!

I FELT AN ALMOST DESPERATE NEED TO BE LOVING TO HER, TO BE THE MOTHER PERHAPS SHE NEVER HAD.

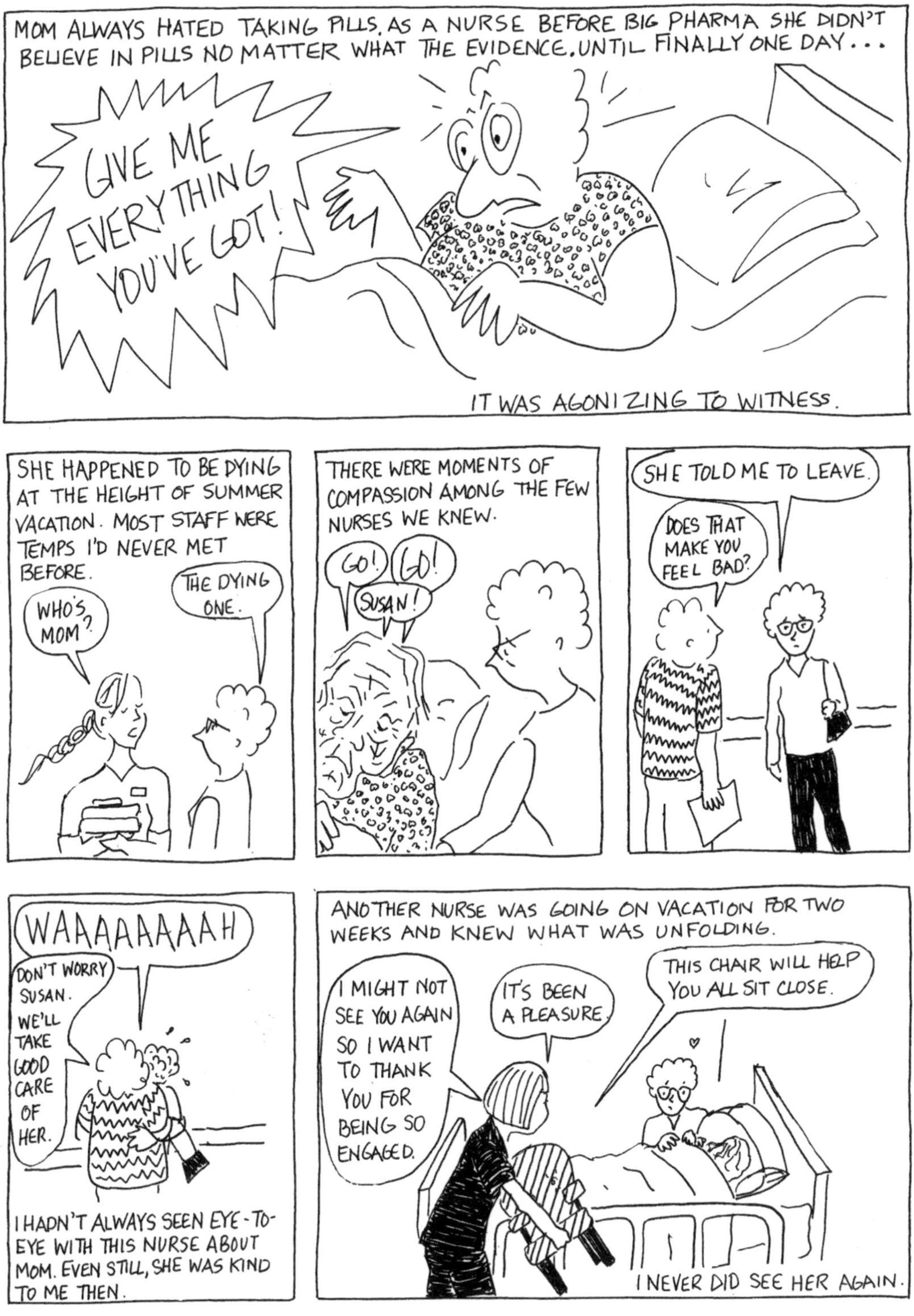
MOM ALWAYS HATED TAKING PILLS. AS A NURSE BEFORE BIG PHARMA SHE DIDN'T BELIEVE IN PILLS NO MATTER WHAT THE EVIDENCE. UNTIL FINALLY ONE DAY...
GIVE ME EVERYTHING YOU'VE GOT!
IT WAS AGONIZING TO WITNESS.
SHE HAPPENED TO BE DYING AT THE HEIGHT OF SUMMER VACATION. MOST STAFF WERE TEMPS I'D NEVER MET BEFORE.
WHO'S MOM?
THE DYING ONE.
THERE WERE MOMENTS OF COMPASSION AMONG THE FEW NURSES WE KNEW.
GO!
GO!
SUSAN!
SHE TOLD ME TO LEAVE.
DOES THAT MAKE YOU FEEL BAD?
WAAAAAAAAH
DON'T WORRY SUSAN. WE'LL TAKE GOOD CARE OF HER.
I HADN'T ALWAYS SEEN EYE-TO-EYE WITH THIS NURSE ABOUT MOM. EVEN STILL, SHE WAS KIND TO ME THEN.
ANOTHER NURSE WAS GOING ON VACATION FOR TWO WEEKS AND KNEW WHAT WAS UNFOLDING.
I MIGHT NOT SEE YOU AGAIN SO I WANT TO THANK YOU FOR BEING SO ENGAGED.
IT'S BEEN A PLEASURE.
THIS CHAIR WILL HELP YOU ALL SIT CLOSE.
I NEVER DID SEE HER AGAIN.

MY BROTHER HAD REASONS FOR NOT COMING. MYSELF I DREADED EACH VISIT. IT FELT LIKE WALKING INTO A FURNACE. THE PAIN WAS SEARING.

WELCOME

ONCE WHEN I WAS SITTING WITH MOM, I BEGAN TO PRAY THAT DEAD RELATIVES SHE LOVED WOULD COME AND GUIDE HER PEACEFULLY.

BUT I COULDN'T THINK OF MANY SHE EXPRESSED LOVE FOR. SHE WAS BIG ON BLAME.

DAD? NO.
QUEENIE? NO!
AUNT LAURA? NO.
AUNT ADA? NO
UMMMM

AUNTIE DAISY!

AUNTIE DAISY WAS QUEENIE'S YOUNGER SISTER AND THE ANTI-QUEENIE. THE FAMILY MAY NOT HAVE CONSIDERED HER "PRETTY", BUT SHE WAS LOVING, KIND, CARING AND GENEROUS. SHE AND MOM WERE ALLIES IN THE FACE OF QUEENIE'S CRUELTIES. FINALLY, DAISY UP AND MOVED TO BOSTON AFTER YEARS LIVING CLOSE.

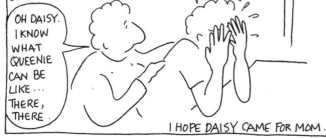

OH DAISY. I KNOW WHAT QUEENIE CAN BE LIKE... THERE, THERE.

I HOPE DAISY CAME FOR MOM.

MOM BECAME VIOLENT AS SHE DECLINED.

YOUR MOTHER'S STARTED SPITTING AT US.

OH, I'M SO SORRY!

IT'S OK. WE'VE SEEN IT BEFORE IN OTHERS.

ONCE, SHORTLY BEFORE SHE TOOK TO HER BED FOR GOOD, I SAW MOM TRYING TO SCRATCH SOMEONE. SHE WAS VICIOUS. STRONG TOO.

THE DIRECTOR OF NURSING TOOK ME ASIDE.

THE ELDERLY CAN REVERT TO CHILDHOOD ACTS THEY USED TO PROTECT THEMSELVES IF THEY WERE ABUSED AS CHILDREN.

WHAA?

QUEENIE?!

THE BODY REMEMBERS!

156

As the days passed, Mom and I had a few brief conversations.

I know... what's... GOING ON!

What's going on, Mom? Do you want to say more?

She shook her head.

And...

I'm very sorry to see you in such pain, Mom.

I love you.

That's so WONDERFUL ...and... so... in... com... pre... ...hensible!

NO!

You're my mother! You deserve my love!

She shook her head.

Mom, whatever you're holding against yourself, please let it go.

No one knows when death will come. It's normal to ask.

Sigh. Families always ask that!

Who teaches them to talk that way?

It turned out Mom died sooner than anyone expected.

I'M DEEPLY COMFORTED THAT MY DAUGHTER HELD MOM'S HAND AND NAPPED WITH HER THE DAY BEFORE SHE DIED.

TRUE TO FORM, THE HOME CALLED ME AT MIDNIGHT AT AN OLD NUMBER, ONE I HAD MADE SURE WAS CORRECTED MONTHS BEFORE.

THE LPN REACHED ME ON MY CELL AROUND 7 AM.

SUSAN, YOUR MOTHER PASSED LAST NIGHT.

I WANTED TO TELL YOU BEFORE THE TEMPS CAME IN.

SHE'LL BE MISSED.

I GOT THE IMPRESSION SHE WAS TICKING-OFF A TO-DO LIST.

AAAAAH

I CALLED EVERYONE I COULD THINK OF.

WE REALLY HAVE TO GO NOW.

AS MY FAMILY ENTERED THE HOME, THE USUALLY FRIENDLY RECEPTIONIST LOOKED THE OTHER WAY. MAYBE NO ONE TOLD HER.

RECEPTIONIST

WE STOOD IN FRONT OF AN LPN I'D NEVER SEEN BEFORE UNTIL SHE REALIZED WE WANTED HER TO TAKE US TO MOM. WE WERE SCARED.

I WAS ASTONISHED AT HOW COLD SHE WAS.

WHEN MOM'S MINISTER ARRIVED, I WEPT IN HIS ARMS WITH A FEROCITY I'D NEVER EXPERIENCED BEFORE. I DIDN'T EXPECT THAT.

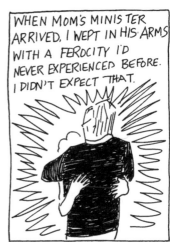

MOM'S MINISTER SAID PRAYERS THEN WE ASKED STAFF TO CALL THE FUNERAL HOME BEFORE WE LEFT. MY DAUGHTER MOTHERED ME.

COME HERE MOM

ONE STAFF MEMBER APPROACHED ME. OTHERS HAD STUFF TO DO I GUESS...

I'M SO SORRY SUSAN. SHE'S NOT IN PAIN NOW. IT'S BETTER.

...THEY LOOKED AWAY.

WHO TEACHES CARE WORKERS NOT TO SPEAK TO PEOPLE LIKE THAT?

THE RESIDENTS, ON THE OTHER HAND, WERE WONDERFUL.

I CAN'T HELP BUT CRY.

SHE'LL BE IN OUR PRAYERS

DEAD!?! YOUR MOTHER? DEAR GOD, THERE'S A LOT OF THAT GOING ON AROUND HERE LATELY.

THE WOMAN WHO SAT AT MOM'S TABLE AND LOATHED US BOTH WAS IN THE HALLWAY.

YOU MONKEY! YOU GET BACK HERE AND BE WITH THAT WICKED WOMAN WHO'S SO SICK.

BUT THAT AFTERNOON WHEN WE WERE CLEANING OUT MOM'S ROOM, SHE CAME TO THE DOOR.

I LOVED HER! I DID! YOU KNOW I DID! I KNOW I CAN BE GRUFF BUT I LOVED HER! I DID!

IT'S OK. IT'S OK, BEV. I KNOW YOU LOVED HER. IT'S OK.

HELP! CAN'T SOMEONE COME AND GET HER?

BUT THE MOST TROUBLING THING THAT DAY WAS LOOKING BACK AT MOM'S BODY AND SEEING HER HAND WAS FROZEN AS IF HOLDING A CALL BELL.

I ARRANGED THE FUNERAL, EULOGIES, RECEPTION AND BURIAL. MY BROTHER CAME LATE THE NIGHT BEFORE THE SERVICE. HE STAYED WITH US OVER THE WEEKEND TO MEET THE BANK MONDAY MORNING. THEN HE LEFT FOR A FEW DAYS FOR HIS FAVORITE DISTANT SHORE WHERE HE...

ALWAYS SPENT MORE TIME DURING HIS VISITS THAN WITH HIS MOTHER!!!

DOESN'T LOOK GOOD ON YOU MOM.

I WAS SURPRISED THAT HE ACTED AS IF THERE WERE NOTHING CHANGED BETWEEN US AFTER OUR VISIT TO THE THERAPIST. ON THE DRIVE BACK FROM THE FUNERAL...

YOUR HOUSE FEELS SO MUCH LIKE HOME. I LOVE IT HERE!

BUT IT'S NEW TO US. HE'S ONLY BEEN IN IT ONCE.

HIS PRESENCE IN THE HOUSE TRIGGERED OLD ANIMOSITIES IN ME.

HE'S GOING TO TAKE STUFF! HE'S ALWAYS TAKING STUFF!

HE'S GOING TO TAKE THE LAST OF OUR BEST CHOCOLATE!

I KNOW THIS EXPOSES SOME TWISTED SISTERNESS.

HE MAY NOT HAVE REALIZED HE WAS DEALING WITH MY WOUNDED CHILD. I DIDN'T REALIZE MOM WAS A WOUNDED CHILD. MAYBE MY BROTHER IS TOO.

IT'S STILL HARD FOR ME TO ACCEPT IT'S NOT PART OF HIS VALUE SYSTEM TO EXPRESS CARING FOR ME IN TIME OF NEED. NOBODY'S FAULT.

JUST HARD FOR ME TO ACCEPT.

HE'S MAKING OFF WITH THIS CHAPTER!

LET'S GET BACK TO MOM!

AT THE FUNERAL
⇒ WE DID HER PROUD ⇐
OUR EULOGIES

BROTHER

I ONCE TRIED TO START CALLING HER BY HER FIRST NAME. SHE QUICKLY DISABUSED ME.

"I WAITED A LONG TIME TO BE CALLED A MOTHER AND YOU'RE NOT TAKING THAT AWAY FROM ME," SHE TOLD ME.

DAUGHTER

I HAVE WARM CHILDHOOD MEMORIES OF BIG HUGS AND KISSES ... SHE TAUGHT ME MANY THINGS INCLUDING THE IMPORTANCE OF NAPPING. IT WAS IMPOSSIBLE FOR US GRANDKIDS TO DISAPPOINT HER. SHE TAUGHT ME NOT TO TAKE THINGS TOO SERIOUSLY... SHE WAS IMPORTANT TO ME AND I WILL MISS HER.

ME

AS I CAME TO LEARN THE WORLD OPENS WHEN YOU EMBRACE VULNERABILITY, WHEN YOUR HEART OPENS ···

I SEE WHAT FOLLY THE WALLS BETWEEN ME AND HER HAD BEEN ···

HER LONG LIFE GAVE ME THE OPPORTUNITY TO SEE MOM'S TRUE NATURE AS ONE OF GENEROSITY AND GOODNESS.

I AM GRATEFUL.

MY GOOD FRIENDS KINDLY ORGANIZED THE FOOD AND MADE SURE THE RECEPTION WENT SMOOTHLY WITH THE HELP OF THE CHURCH WOMEN. MY COUSINS ATTENDED IN FORCE.

DID ANYONE BRING A CORKSCREW?

MOM LOVED SHERRY AND MY BROTHER RAISED A TOAST.

TO MARJORIE!

AN OLDER RELATIVE WHO HAD BEEN AROUND WHILE WE WERE BEING RAISED TURNED TO ME AT ONE POINT...

OH! YOUR MOTHER LOOOVED YOU!

IT WASN'T SOMETHING I HAD EVER FELT.

I DO NOW. FROM MY EULOGY...

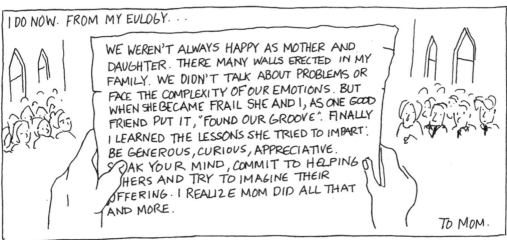

WE WEREN'T ALWAYS HAPPY AS MOTHER AND DAUGHTER. THERE MANY WALLS ERECTED IN MY FAMILY. WE DIDN'T TALK ABOUT PROBLEMS OR FACE THE COMPLEXITY OF OUR EMOTIONS. BUT WHEN SHE BECAME FRAIL SHE AND I, AS ONE GOOD FRIEND PUT IT, "FOUND OUR GROOVE". FINALLY I LEARNED THE LESSONS SHE TRIED TO IMPART: BE GENEROUS, CURIOUS, APPRECIATIVE. SPEAK YOUR MIND, COMMIT TO HELPING OTHERS AND TRY TO IMAGINE THEIR SUFFERING. I REALIZE MOM DID ALL THAT AND MORE.

TO MOM.

CHAPTER THIRTEEN

WHAT'S LEFT TO SAY?

TWICE IN THE WEEK FOLLOWING MOM'S FUNERAL, A HUMMINGBIRD VISITED OUR DECK. WE HADN'T SEEN ONE BEFORE. NOR SINCE. I LIKE TO THINK...

BYE MOM.

AFTER THE FUNERAL, I CORNERED MY BROTHER AS WE WENT THROUGH MOM'S PAPERS.

WE NEED TO TALK ABOUT OUR RELATIONSHIP.

?

WHEN YOU CONFIRMED THIS WALL IS BETWEEN US, I WAS HURT AND ANGRY.

I DIDN'T SAY THAT.

YOU DID.

I WENT BACK TO THE THERAPIST AND WE WENT OVER THE CONVERSATION.

YOU TOOK IT OUT OF CONTEXT.

HOW?

I DIDN'T HEAR AN ANSWER. INSTEAD I HEARD MORE ABOUT HOW HARD HIS LIFE IS.

GRRR

MORE DEFLECTION?

DESPITE THIS... I THINK WE SHOULD TRY AND HAVE A RELATIONSHIP. MOM WOULD HAVE WANTED THAT.

WE TALKED AND DREW UP AN AGREEMENT. WE SIGNED IT. WE AGREED WE WOULD BOTH TAKE THE INITIATIVE.

WE AGREE... ♥

♥

WE BOTH WANT TO BUILD LOVING TRUST WITH EACH OTHER. ♥ ♥

FOR SISTER, THAT MEANS OPEN, HONEST COMMUNICATIONS WHEN THINGS BOTHER US.

♥

FOR BROTHER THAT MEANS A NEED TO FEEL ACCEPTANCE AND NON-JUDGEMENT VS EXPECTATIONS AND "SHOULDS".

♥

FOR BOTH, THAT MEANS SEEKING UNDERSTANDING, ASKING QUESTIONS THAT ARE ANSWERED HONESTLY, RESPECTFULLY.

AT THE BANK THE NEXT DAY, JUST BEFORE HE LEFT, WE SPOKE WHILE THE MANAGER MADE PHOTOCOPIES.

IN MY BOOK, I'M GOING TO TALK ABOUT SIBLING RIVALRY AS PARENTS DECLINE.

THERE ARE WORSE RIVALRIES THAN OURS.

SOME SIBLINGS STEAL.

UMM, I DIDN'T UNDERSTAND WHY YOU NEEDED THE PAID VISITOR UNTIL RECENTLY. AND YOU HAVE A LOT OF FRIENDS. I DIDN'T KNOW YOU WERE LONELY FOR ME UNTIL THE THERAPIST

WELL, WHY DIDN'T YOU ASK ME?

I REALIZE NOW THIS IS A "SHOULD"

AND JUST WHO TAUGHT ME TO TALK THAT WAY?

AFTER HE LEFT, I FOUND HE HADN'T TAKEN HIS COPY OF THE AGREEMENT. I DIDN'T BOTHER SENDING IT. HE DIDN'T ASK FOR IT.

HUH?

THUNK!

THE SOUND OF US EACH PUTTING BACK A BRICK.

I HAD ALWAYS SENT HIM CHRISTMAS GREETINGS FROM MOM AND ME. I FIGURED SINCE I HAD TAKEN THE INITIATIVE ON **EVERYTHING**, HE WOULD SEND ME A CARD THAT YEAR.

WRONG!

I BECAME UNSEASONAL AGAIN.

AND MISTAKEN AGAIN. THE THERAPIST EXPLAINED WHY.

BASICALLY, IT IS INEFFECTIVE TO EXPECT OTHERS TO BEHAVE AS YOU THINK THEY SHOULD.

IT'S EMOTIONALLY EXHAUSTING. THINKING AND BELIEVING IN "SHOULD" STATEMENTS ONLY CAUSES YOU MORE SUFFERING.

SIGH.

THE ONLY THING WE CONTROL IS OURSELVES.

THERE WILL ALWAYS BE PAIN BUT THERE DOESN'T NEED TO BE SUFFERING.

MY BROTHER SENT GREETINGS AND A DAVID WHYTE POEM ON MY FEBRUARY BIRTHDAY.

LOVELY

I DON'T UNDERSTAND WHAT THE HELL HE'S COMMUNICATING WITH THIS POEM.

HE REPLIED WITH A LONG EMAIL ABOUT HIS RECENT ACCOMPLISHMENTS AND THAT HE'D BE BACK IN A FEW SUMMERS.

I COULDN'T BRING MYSELF TO WRITE, "LOOKING FORWARD."

SINCE THEN I'VE REPLIED TO HIS EMAILS WHICH ARE ONLY ABOUT HIS ACCOMPLISHMENTS WITH...

GOOD FOR YOU!

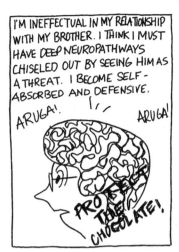

I'M INEFFECTUAL IN MY RELATIONSHIP WITH MY BROTHER. I THINK I MUST HAVE DEEP NEUROPATHWAYS CHISELED OUT BY SEEING HIM AS A THREAT. I BECOME SELF-ABSORBED AND DEFENSIVE.

ARUGA!

ARUGA!

PROTECT THE CHOCOLATE!

INTELLECTUALLY, I CAN REASON WITH MYSELF, BUT EMOTIONALLY...

MAYBE HIS LIFE REALLY IS HARD.

MAYBE HE'S LOOKING FOR ADMIRATION AND APPROVAL FROM ME AND I'M LOOKING FOR CARE AND CONCERN FROM HIM.

AND WE CAN'T GENUINELY GIVE THEM TO EACH OTHER BECAUSE WE FEEL WE NEVER RECEIVED THEM AS CHILDREN.

OR MAYBE HE SHOULDN'T EXIST!

IT'S AN INNER BATTLE.

RIGHT AFTER THE FUNERAL, I CHATTED WITH A GOOD FRIEND.

SO, YOU SAW MY BROTHER AT THE FUNERAL. SPAWN OF THE DEVIL, EH?

HA! HA! HA! SUSAN, HE SEEMS LIKE MOST MEN TO ME. OBLIVIOUS!

I KNOW HE'S A GOOD PERSON, A DECENT HUMAN BEING. BUT I HAVE SUCH A VISCERAL REACTION TO HIM. I'M MY VERY WORST SELF AROUND HIM! I'M ANGRY AT HIM FOR THAT TOO!

OH, I KNOW! IT'S THE SAME WITH MY SIBLINGS. I CAN GO RIGHT BACK TO CHILDHOOD WITH THEM IN AN INSTANCE!

IT'S PAINFUL.

AND LONELY.

I OFTEN WONDER WHY I WAS DRIVEN TO WRITE THIS MEMOIR.

USUALLY, IT'S TO GO BACK AND RECOVER SOME LOST ASPECT OF THE PAST SO IT CAN BE INTEGRATED INTO CURRENT IDENTITY.

ART OF MEMOIR MARY KARR

THAT, AND I WANTED TO COMMUNICATE SO MUCH. PERHAPS THIS BOOK IS ALSO AN ATTEMPT TO TELL MY STORY TO MY BROTHER. MAYBE WE'VE BOTH DONE MEAN THINGS BUT NEITHER OF US HAS A MEAN DISPOSITION.

PERHAPS I WANT MY BROTHER TO KNOW I LOVE HIM AT SOME LEVEL.

MY COMMUNICATIONS ATTEMPTS FAILED WITH THE NURSING HOME, GOVERNMENT AND MY BROTHER.

BUT NOT WITH MOM.

I WAS NAIVE TO THINK THAT COMMUNICATIONS FROM US TWO WOULD BE HEARD BY OTHERS.

GOVERNMENT

BROTHER

NURSING HOME

WHAT SALLIE TISDALE SAYS ABOUT COMMUNICATIONS MAKES SENSE.

SUSAN & SEEKS AN EXPERT

WHY IS COMMUNICATIONS SO HARD FOR HUMANS?

WELL... LANGUAGE IS LITTLE MORE THAN THE DEMILITARIZED ZONE IN WHICH WE TRY TO NEGOTIATE SOME UNSTABLE PEACE.

COMMUNICATIONS IS THE SECOND SELF, OR THIRD, ALWAYS FALSE; THE FIRST ONE COWERS OR CRIES OUT.

MY FIRST SELF CRIES OUT!

WHAT SHE SAYS ABOUT FAMILIES ALSO RESONATES WITH ME.

FAMILY, FOR MOST OF US, INCLUDES LIFELONG AGREEMENTS ABOUT WHAT IS NOT SAID. THE FEAR OF HUMILIATION . . . IS STRONG.

BETWEEN SIBLINGS, THERE ARE NO VOWS, NO CONTRACTS, NO PROMISES. IT IS SO GODDAMNED DANGEROUS TO LOVE!

WE ARE NEVER VISIBLE TO OTHERS EXACTLY, NOR IS THE WORLD WHOLLY VISIBLE TO US; THE SHELL IS ALWAYS THERE IN BETWEEN.

I LOVE YOU, SALLIE!

I'VE HEARD THAT FORGIVENESS IS LETTING GO OF A RESENTMENT THAT'S ENTITLED. FORGIVENESS RARELY COMES EASILY, CERTAINLY NOT INSTANTLY.

AGREEMENT: WE AGREE.

DOOMED TO BUILD LOVING TRU WITH

MY CONFLICT WITH MY BROTHER TAUGHT ME SO MUCH, MOSTLY ABOUT MYSELF.

I DON'T HAVE TO HOLD HIM IN MY HEART WITH ANGER?

WHILE I CAN BETTER SEE MY ROLE IN OUR CONFLICT, I NOW KNOW THAT I DON'T HAVE TO KEEP BEATING MYSELF UP FOR BEING A MEAN OLDER SISTER.

WOW.

IN PART, I CAME TO REALIZE THIS IN A CONFLICT COURSE I TOOK.

WHEN YOU'RE DEALING WITH SOMEONE YOU DISLIKE OR MISTRUST, DO IT WITH GREAT LOVE.

YOU'RE STEPPING INTO THE RIVER OF SOMEONE ELSE'S LIFE AND THEN STEPPING OUT.

BE HUMBLE.

EMPOWERED COMMUNICATIONS . . . SPEAKING YOUR TRUTH WITH COMPASSION.

TRY TO REPLACE CLOSED-MINDED JUDGEMENT WITH CURIOSITY AND OPEN-MINDEDNESS.

BUT, TAKE CARE OF YOURSELF. WE TAKE CARE OF OTHERS NOT AT THE EXPENSE OF OURSELVES. WE TAKE CARE OF OURSELVES NOT AT THE EXPENSE OF OTHERS.

MY BROTHER TURNED OUT TO BE MY ZEN TEACHER.

HIS BRICK WALL BECAME A MIRROR. I COULD REFLECT ON MY REFLECTION...

UGH.

...AND LEARN TO FORGIVE MYSELF AS WELL BECAUSE I'M NOT UNIQUE.

THIS IS WHAT IT MEANS TO LEAD A HUMAN LIFE.

EVERYONE HAS PAIN IN WAYS SIMILAR TO THIS.

I'VE SLOWLY LEARNED TO TAKE A BIGGER PERSPECTIVE ON IT ALL.

BUZZ I'M PEEING! BUZZ WTF?!

UNINTENDED IMPACTS FEAR PATRIARCHY ENTRENCHED SYSTEMS SHAME HUMAN NATURE POLITICS FAMILY STUFF

ECONOMIC VALUES AGEISM OUTDATED HIERARCHIES SOCIETAL DOUBLE-TALK

VULNERABILITY

IT'S HARD TO SEE A CLEAR WAY THROUGH THIS. AND I HAD PRIVILEGE. I WAS LUCKY!

I ALSO LEARNED I CAN SHOW UP IN WAYS THAT FEEL RIGHT TO ME. I CAN BE AN ADULT AND STILL PROTECT MY WOUNDED CHILD.

IT'S OK TO FEEL WHAT YOU FEEL.

JUST LET ME DO THE TALKING.

I KNOW TOO I WILL FAIL IN TRYING TO COME TO BETTER TERMS WITH MY BROTHER WITHIN MYSELF. IT'S AN INSIDE JOB, AND IT TAKES PRACTICE.

YIKES! COME BACK!

SELF-COMPASSION IS KEY WHEN I FEEL TRIGGERED BY HIM.

MAY I BE KIND TO MYSELF.

MAY I HAVE PEACE.

MAY I ACCEPT MYSELF AS I AM.

THAT SEEMS TO SOFTEN INTERNAL WALLS A BIT AND OPEN POSSIBILITIES.

A GOOD THERAPIST HELPED MAKE SENSE OF THINGS TOO.

EACH GENERATION, IF GIVEN THE SKILLS, CAN BE MORE EFFECTIVE THAN THEIR PARENTS AND CHANGE HOW THEY WANT TO PARENT.

WELL, I KNOW I'VE MADE A LOT OF MISTAKES AS A PARENT.

MAYBE MY KIDS WILL GET IT RIGHT.

A DAILY MEDITATION PRACTICE HELPS ME UNDERSTAND MY SELF-DELUSIONS—SOMEWHAT.

THE WISDOM OF MY HAIRDRESSER HELPED TOO.

WHEN THE MATRIARCH DIES, IF THE CHILDREN HAVEN'T BEEN CLOSE, THEY WON'T BE NOW.

BE POLITE, BUT DON'T LET HIM TAKE ADVANTAGE.

YOU HAVE YOUR OWN FAMILY. HE'S NOT REALLY YOUR FAMILY.

LET HIM GO WITH LOVE.

HEY YOU! MAY ALL YOUR DEEPEST DREAMS BE REALIZED. MAY YOU BE SAFE AND HEALTHY. MAY YOU HAVE LOVE, LIGHT AND LAUGHTER IN YOUR LIFE. (JUST DON'T INVOLVE ME.)

I'M TRYING, OK!

THERE'S NOT MUCH I CAN DO ABOUT AGEISM IN SOCIETY.

HEY! STOP RUNNING AWAY FROM AGING!

IT'S UNLIKELY I'll BE ABLE TO CHANGE THE VALUES OUR ECONOMY IS BASED UPON.

INTERNATIONAL MONETARY FUND

WELCOME!

THERE'S LOTS TO DREAD ABOUT OLD AGE.

I FEAR BEING ISOLATED, LEFT OUT, MY WORK BECOMING IRRELEVANT.

I FEAR BEING IN PAIN.

YET I ALSO KNOW THERE ARE THINGS I CAN LOOK FORWARD TO IN MY OLD AGE.

FACT: THE ELDERLY HAVE COMFORT WITH AMBIGUITY, AND HAVE DEEPER GRATITUDE AND GREATER COMPASSION.

FACT: HAPPINESS AT 90 FAR EXCEEDS THAT AT 18.

YAY! CAN'T WAIT!

I KNOW THAT I CAN TRY TO GO INTO AGING WITH OPEN EYES, A KIND ATTITUDE AND CONTINUE ADVOCATING FOR JUST POLICY.

MAYBE ALL OUR PRIOR YEARS ARE PRACTICING FOR THE HARD STUFF OF GROWING OLD.

ANTICIPATE, ADAPT, ACCEPT.

THE ROOT MEANING OF THE WORD "COMPASSION" IS "TO SUFFER WITH". I DRAW PEOPLE IN NURSING HOMES, IN PART TO SHOW THEIR SUFFERING...

I'M NOT VISITED MUCH. NOT SURE WHERE MY SON IS NOW.

... AND THEIR HUMANITY

YOU CAN DRAW ME LIKE THIS! (GIGGLES)

ALWAYS HAD DOGS. MOSTLY MEDIUM. I'M TOO SMALL FOR BIG ONES.

YOU ARE BEAUTIFUL!

DRIVE ME?! DRAW YOU?! OH, DRAW ME! YES, DEAR, YES. (chuckling.)

OF COURSE, THERE ARE NURSING HOMES THAT GIVE EXCELLENT CARE. I'VE SEEN IT.

YOU TIRED? YOUR BACK SORE? WE'LL GET YOU BACK TO BED AFTER SUPPER.

AS THE END OF THIS BOOK NEARS, I TURN TO MY FINAL EXPERT.

SUSAN SEEKS AN EXPERT

>ME!<

WELL, SOLUTION SUSAN, WHAT CAN WE TAKE AWAY FROM YOUR EXPERIENCE?

UMMM . . .

SOLUTION SUSAN STRIKES

I SHOULD BE HESITANT TO GIVE ADVICE — I NOW KNOW BETTER — BUT BEING ME...

WELL, BE KIND TO YOURSELF BUT...

DON'T LET YOURSELF OFF THE HOOK. BE KIND TO OTHERS BUT SET BOUNDARIES.

SOMETIMES PEOPLE CAN'T OR WON'T MEET YOU HALF-WAY. DON'T OVERREACH.

TRY AND BE AWARE OF THE IMPACT OF YOUR ACTIONS AND NON-ACTIONS.

NOTE WHO YOU IGNORE AND AVOID, WHO YOU BLAME AND WHY.

ASK YOURSELF, HOW CAN I BE THE BEST VERSION OF MYSELF WHEN I'M TRIGGERED BY SOMETHING I FIND PAINFUL OR JUDGE HARSHLY?

AT THE SAME TIME, TRYING TOO HARD TO CONTROL HOW WE THINK, FEEL, AND BEHAVE GETS IN THE WAY OF LIVING.

STILL, TRY PAYING ATTENTION TO THE VULNERABLE PEOPLE NEAREST YOU, WHETHER OR NOT YOU KNOW THEM. THE VULNERABLE NEED YOU TO SEE THEIR HUMANITY. THEY'LL SHOW YOU THEIRS.

AND YOURS.

UNDERSTAND WE'RE ALL LIVING LIVES REACTING TO THE INHERITED INJUSTICE OF THE PAST. TRY AND RECOGNIZE THIS IN YOURSELF AND OTHERS.

OF COURSE I'M ONLY TALKING TO MYSELF. IF I'VE LEARNED ANYTHING IT'S THAT...

...WHEN MY EFFORTS AREN'T HELPFUL, SADLY ALL I CAN DO IS...

GENTLY REFLECT

ACCEPT,

AND

PAY ATTENTION,

ALWAYS.

END NOTES AND SOURCES

Much of my research comes from Dr. Louise Aronson whose book *Elderhood: Redefining Aging, Transforming Medicine, Reimagining Life* is imperative for anyone interested in seeing and facing old age with more generosity, more kindness. Very readable. https://louisearonson.com/ (Bloomsbury Publishing: New York, 2019).

Chapter Five: Decoding Elder-World Language: What's Really Being Sold

Page 69: Chris Power was CEO of the former Capital District Health Authority in Nova Scotia, 2006-2015 and confirmed this content. Peter MacDougall, a recently retired health services manager with the Nova Scotia Health Authority, helped me ensure this perspective of the role is accurate.

Page 70: Phone interview with Graham Steele, November 5, 2020. He was a member of the Nova Scotia legislature from 2001 to 2013 and the minister of finance between 2009 and 2012. He is the author of *The Effective Citizen: How to Make Politicians Work for You* (Nimbus Publishing: Halifax, Nova Scotia, 2017).

Page 72: Philippe Leonard Fradet, "4 Ways Men Can Take on More Emotional Labor in Relationships (And Why We Should)," thebodyisnotanapology.com/magazine, May 28, 2019.

Chapter Six: Nothing's Wrong Here.

Page 80: **they're like children** A nursing home resident's paid visitor said this to me. Over the years I began to realize how true this was. **2.45 hours of care per resident per day** Louise Riley (contributed) "Proper staffing ratios in long-term care make a world of difference," https://www.saltwire.com/halifax/opinion/local-perspectives/louise-riley-proper-staffing-ratios-in-long-term-care-make-a-world-of-difference-458775/, June 8, 2020; Also, Long-Term Care Staffing Study, https://www.ontario.ca/page/long-term-care-staffing-study#section-4: "We urge the ministry to move towards a minimum daily average of four hours of direct care per resident as quickly as possible." (In Nova Scotia, the 2.45 ratio of care/per resident/per day is not tied to quality of care, just licensing.)

Page 83: Marie-Claire Chartrand owns Greywave Senior Care Consulting, Halifax, Nova Scotia. https://greywave.ca/. Last panel: Vincent Lam, "André Picard's new book *Neglected No More* examines the disorganization of eldercare in Canada," Special to *The Globe and Mail*, https://www.theglobeandmail.com/arts/books/reviews/article-andre-picards-new-book-neglected-no-more-examines-the-disorganization/, March 4, 2021.

Chapter Seven: People, Eh?

Page 92: **the department of health and wellness provides a budget:** correspondence between me and then Director, Liaison and Service Support, Continuing Care Branch, Department of Health and Wellness, Nova Scotia.

Page 93: My supportive friend is Dr. Deborah McLeod, who at the time was a clinician scientist in nursing/psychosocial oncology at the QEII Cancer Care program in Halifax, Nova Scotia.

Page 97: Thomas R Cole, "A Job I Never Expected" Oxford University Press Blog, https://blog.oup.com/2020/01/a-job-i-never-expected/, January 6, 2020.

Page 100: Liz O'Donnell, "The Crisis Facing America's Working Daughters," *The Atlantic*, February 9, 2016. She quotes Anne Tumlinson, an American expert in setting aging and disability policy. She is founder of the caregiver support website, https://www.daughterhood.org/.

Chapter Eight: So Hard.

Page 102, last panel: All resident names have been changed for confidentiality.

Page 104: **alarm fatigue** Kathleen Gaines, "Alarm Fatigue is Way Too Real (and Scary) For Nurses," https://nurse.org/articles/alarm-fatigue-statistics-patient-safety/, August 19, 2019; **some suggest biomedical engineers** Igual, R., Medrano, C. & Plaza, I. "Challenges, issues and trends in fall detection systems." *BioMed Eng OnLine 12*, 66 (2013) https://doi.org/10.1186/1475-925X-12-66

Page 105: Dr. Robin Youngson, *Time to Care: How to Love Your Patients and Your Job* (Rebelheart Publishers: New Zealand, 2012) 8.

Page 106: Interview with Saphia Cunningham, Saint Vincent's Nursing Home, Halifax, Nova Scotia; Also, "Currently, about 80 percent of shifts in care homes and home care are not fully staffed . . .", André Picard, *Neglected No More: The Urgent Need to Improve the Lives of Canada's Elders in the Wake of a Pandemic* (Random House Canada: Toronto, 2021) 165.

Page 107: Armstrong, Pat, and Ruth Lowndes, ed., *Negotiating Tensions in Long-Term Residential Care: Ideas Worth Sharing* (RR Donnelley: Montreal, 2018) 45 ; panel six **this explains how funders** Stephanie Nolan, "What Happened at Northwood: How Nova Scotia Failed Its Most Vulnerable," *The Coast: Halifax Uncovered*, April 22, 2021.

Page 108: **you use the term "capitalist clock"** 2020 email correspondence with Dr. Jared Gardner, Director, Popular Culture Studies, Billy Ireland Cartoon Library & Museum and Joseph V. Denney Designated Professor of English, The Ohio State University; panel 3: John Ibbitson, "In This Aging Society, Canada Needs More Female Leaders for Everyone's Sake," *The Globe and Mail*, February 21, 2020.

Page 111: Moira Welsh, *Happily Ever Older: Revolutionary Approaches to Long-Term Care*, (ECW Press: Toronto, 2021) 12.

Page 112: Youngson, *Time to Care*, 17.

Page 113: **the quality of relational care among siblings** Unattributed, "The Dynamics of Sibling Caregiving (with Video)," https://www.caregiverstress.com/family-communication/solving-family-conflict/dynamics-sibling-caregiving-video/, Home Instead Senior Care website, June 2017.

Chapter Nine: Going South Fast

Page 117: Sallie Tisdale, *Advice for Future Corpses: A Practical Perspective on Death and Dying* (Gallery Books: New York, 2018) 94.

Page 120: R.M. Vaughan, "What to expect when your parent is dying," *The Globe and Mail,* January 1, 2015. Mr. Vaughan, novelist and playwright, wrote a series of columns for *The Globe and Mail* about the impact his mother's dying and death had on him and his brother.

Page 122: Dr. Francine Russo, https://francinerusso.com/ quoted in Zosia Bielski, "Caring for elderly parents inflames old sibling rivalries," *The Globe and Mail*, February 8, 2010.

Chapter Ten: Talking About Families

Page 130: Jennifer Hunter, "Cain's Legacy: Liberating siblings from a lifetime of rage, shame, secrecy and regret." *Toronto Star*, February 11, 2012; Panel 6, 7, 8: Ken MacQueen, "Why It's Not Your Fault You Can't Stand Your Sibling," *Maclean's*, January 18, 2012. (An interview with Jeanne Safer.)

Page 132: Christine Hutchison, "Why Women Are Tired: The Price of Unpaid Emotional Labor," http://www.psychedinsanfrancisco.com, April 7, 2017.

Page 136: Brené Brown, *Daring Greatly: How the Courage to Be Vulnerable Transforms the Way We Live, Love, Parent, and Lead*, (Avery: New York, 2012) 105.

Page 137: Louise Aronson, *Elderhood: Redefining Aging, Transforming Medicine, Reimagining Life* (Bloomsbury Publishing: New York, 2019) 70.

Page 138: Thich Nhat Hanh, *Chanting From The Heart: Buddhist Ceremonies and Daily Practices* (Parallax Press: Berkeley, California, 2007) 76; John Halliday, ed. *Don't Bring Me No Rocking Chair: Poems on Aging* (Tyne and Wear, UK: Bloodaxe Book Ltd, 2014) 187.

Chapter Eleven: Stick Around and Old Will Find You.

Page 140: Otto Von Busch, "The Fashion Fantasy," *Lion's Roar* magazine, July 2020.

Page 141: Telephone interview with Dr. Liesl Gambold, anthropologist, Department of Sociology and Social Anthropology, Dalhousie University, Halifax, Nova Scotia, April 23, 2020; Brian Bethune, "Leaning Out," *Maclean's*, May 1, 2020, interview with Tara Henley.

Page 142: email interview with Graham Steele, November 5, 2020.

Page 143: Louise Aronson, *Elderhood: Redefining Aging, Transforming Medicine, Re-imagining Life*. (Bloomsbury Publishing: New York, 2019), 70, 395, 398, 399.

Page 146: Leigh, J Paul et al. "Physician career satisfaction within specialties." BMC health services research vol. 9, 166. 16 Sep. 2009, doi:10.1186/1472-6963-9-166; Page 8: Hippocratic oath: Aronson, *Elderhood*, 158.

Page 148: **Justice in policy:** Aronson, *Elderhood*, 93; Kenny: Interview with Russell Brand on *Under The Skin* podcast #40, June 11, 2017, https://www.youtube.com/watch?v=Zj7j283AFWY; Rebecca Solnit, *The Mother of All Questions: Further Reports from the Feminist Revolutions*, (Haymarket Books: Chicago, 2017) 36, 142.

Chapter Twelve: No One Gets Out Alive

Page 156: An Executive Director from a different nursing home told me that staff should never have implied that Mom's behaviour was due to childhood abuse. She said there are other conditions that could cause this behaviour. "Dumbass thing to say," were, I believe, her exact words.

Chapter Thirteen: What's Left to Say?

Much of the thinking in this chapter is indebted to *"The Reality Slap: Finding Peace and Fulfillment When Life Hurts"* (New Harbinger Publications, Inc.: Oakland, CA, 2012).

Page 170: Sallie Tisdale, *Violations: Collected Essays*, (Hawthorne Books: Portland, Oregon, 2016) 353.

Page 171: Sallie Tisdale, *Violations*, 314, 317; Basia Solarz, **when you're dealing with someone you dislike** Resource Guide, "Empowered Communication: Speaking Your Truth with Compassion" workshop, based on material from the Institute for the Study of Conflict Transformation, 2020.

Page 174: Aronson, *Elderhood*, 255; Margit Cox Henderson, "The Paradox of Aging: The Happiness U-Curve," March 2018; Ellyn A. Lem, "Often, the elderly handle the pandemic very well. Here's why," *The Washington Post*, September 19, 2020.

Photo: Grace Allen

ACKNOWLEDGEMENTS

One pen stroke after another, bit by bit, brought this book to life. It's been a long haul.

Colleen MacIsaac was always there beside me, if not in body then in spirit during COVID, with a gently critical eye and a kind hand that picked me up and pointed me in the right direction whenever needed.

Angela Berrette, Nancy Maguire and the volunteer board at Saint Vincent's Nursing Home trusted me with their residents, and I relied upon them as a resource. They were not my mother's home; rather they showed me how caring could be given despite the obstacles inherent to long term care.

I owe a huge debt to the Master of Fine Arts in Creative Nonfiction program at the University of King's College. Don Sedgewick believed in the project long before I did. Kim Pittaway is a master of creative-midwifery while mentors Harry Thurston, Jane Silicot and Rebecca Roher were always deeply thoughtful and honest in their feedback. My fellow students remain inspiring, and I am humbled to be among their company. Thank you, Karalee Clerk, for pointing me in this direction.

Andy Brown at Conundrum Press took a chance on me even though I didn't know the very basics of cartooning ("What's inking?"). Sarah Sawler helped me promote the book with fun and enthusiasm. The Center for Cartoon Studies in Vermont is ideal for anyone wanting a solid background in the how-tos as well as the whys and what-not-tos and, if I had found them sooner, I wouldn't have embarrassed myself as often.

The Suppergettes cheered me on and offered wine, gin, and food at high and low moments. My non-birth-but-dear-sister, Kathy MacCulloch, was there for me steadfastly before, during and long after my mother's death. This is simply what she does for many people when they're in need. Peter MacDougall took the time to make sure I understood what health services managers are up against.

Diane Wooden didn't flinch from the craziness I expressed about my brother. She had time and advice for me at my most off-kilter.

My relationship with my brother taught me oh so much about myself and relationships. Without him, there would have been little growth. I hope there's more serenity in our future. Thank you, Mom, for being you and being there.

Canada Council for the Arts and Arts Nova Scotia were both generous in their support. Canada may not be a wonderful place to age, but it is a wonderful place to be creative.

I've talked and corresponded with many people about long term care and sibling relationships in the course of this book's delivery and read many works. Please know any errors or omissions are mine alone.

My immediate family cares about me a lot and that's the most profound comfort in the world. I married a kind and intelligent man many years ago and without him I would not be me.

THINGS TO KNOW IF YOU HAVE A LOVED ONE ENTERING LONG TERM CARE.

- Communications with staff can be difficult. Be patient and persistent, friendly and frank.
- You will be an emotional basket case : Sadness, anger, relief, guilt, frustration, you name it.
- Staff can be wonderful.
- Staff can be nasty.
- Residents can be wonderful.
- Residents can be nasty.
- Families can be wonderful.
- Families can be nasty.

> I DON'T WANT TO MAKE THE BEST OF IT!

- Be there regularly! If you leave them there alone, they may be left there alone.
- You will still be the primary caregiver. You will need to engage with your loved one, shop for them, take them out, even help feed them from time to time.

- Be friendly with other residents. Speak to them regularly. They may long for attention. You may even be supporting and volunteering with them sometimes.

- Few people, even some staff, **WANT** to be in a nursing home. Your positive attention will help.
- You may choose to advocate for system change!
- You may find yourself valuing this meaningful experience.
- There will be death.